The Unholy
in Holy Scripture

Also by Gerd Lüdemann
Published by Westminster John Knox Press

Heretics: The Other Side of Early Christianity
What Really Happened to Jesus: A Historical Approach to the Resurrection

The Unholy
in Holy Scripture
The Dark Side of the Bible

GERD LÜDEMANN

Translated and with an appendix
by John Bowden

Westminster John Knox Press
· Louisville, Kentucky

Translated by John Bowden from the German
Das Unheilige in der Heiligen Schrift: Die andere Seite der Bibel,
published 1996 by Radius Verlag, Stuttgart.

© Radius Verlag 1996
Translation © John Bowden 1997

Cover design by Alec Bartsch
Cover photograph courtesy of PNI Ltd.

First published 1997 by
SCM Press Ltd, London

First American edition 1997
Published by Westminster John Knox Press
Louisville, Kentucky

This book is printed on acid-free paper that meets the
American National Standards Institute Z39.48 standard. ∞

PRINTED IN THE UNITED STATES OF AMERICA
97 98 99 00 01 02 03 04 05 06 — 10 9 8 7 6 5 4 3 2 1

Library of Congress Cataloging-in-Publication Data

Lüdemann, Gerd.
    [Unheilige in der Heiligen Schrift. English]
    The unholy in Holy Scripture : the dark side of the Bible / Gerd
Lüdemann ; translated, and with and appendix by John Bowden. — 1st
American ed.
            p.   cm.
    Includes bibliographical references and index.
    ISBN 0-664-25739-9 (alk. paper)
    1. Bible—Controversial literature.   2. Bible—Criticism,
interpretation, etc.   I. Title.
BS533.L8313   1997
220.6—dc21   96-52254

In memory of Anne Potter Wilson
1921–1986

Contents

Preface to the English Edition

No other book is printed as often as the Bible, no other book has been translated into so many languages and no other book has aimed at so great an influence. Without it there would be no Western culture and no Christian church. Nevertheless the content of the Bible is largely unknown and its use by the Christian churches, to which at present around two billion people belong, is highly selective. Still, it is universally regarded as the Word of God.

But what about those parts of the Bible which contain God's command to exterminate whole peoples? Moreover, what are we to say about texts of the Bible which demonize those of other faiths?

The present book seeks to investigate these groups of problems and to bring out the suppressed heritage of the Bible with ruthless honesty. It brings together observations and formulates questions which have been of burning interest to me ever since I began to read the Bible and engage in scholarly research into it. But above all the book seeks quite simply to inform and to provide an introduction to the suppressed pages of the Bible.

That there is some polemic in the book against officials of the Protestant Church in Germany arises from the fact that since the publication of my books *The Resurrection of Jesus* (1994) and *Heretics* (1996) I have been exposed to increasingly sharp attacks from this quarter. The book itself is an indirect answer to these attacks. To illustrate the substance of them I have therefore prefaced the main part of the book with the text of an interview which highlights the chief points of the controversy. I am grateful to the editors of *Evangelische Kommentare* for permission to include this.

English-speaking readers may be unfamiliar with two documents to which I refer: (*a*) the Preface to Holy Scripture by Eduard Lohse, which has been prefixed to the revised Luther Bible of 1984 (see 5 below); (*b*) the memorandum of the Protestant Church in Germany on *Believing Today. Becoming a Christian and Remaining a Christian* of 1988 (see 23f. below). However, since the doctrines of the authority and use of the Bible expressed in these documents can be paralleled almost precisely in similar documents produced by the churches in England and North America, I have left the sections discussing them unchanged in the text.

I have also cited many sources in this work, in order to arouse the curiosity of readers in the subjects it discusses. Where biblical texts have been cited, as a rule the translation of the RSV has been used.

At all phases of the composition of the book, Silke Röthke and Frank Schleritt have given their well-tested help; Marita Hübner has worked out philosophical questions and with Martina Janssen, Alf Özen and Jürgen Wehnert has read through the completed manuscript. I am grateful to them all for their constructive work, numerous suggestions for improvement and generous criticism. I am also grateful to Eugene TeSelle for reading through the English translation and making useful comments.

The appendix written by my friend John Bowden, which I have asked him to include, may serve as a general introduction to the topic of the book and gives me the hope that historical reconstruction and understanding will continue to remain indispensable in the third millennium.

London, October 1996   Gerd Lüdemann

Jesus the Sinner

An Interview with *Evangelische Kommentare* (October 1995)

Professor Lüdemann, already for some time there has been renewed interest in the person of Jesus of Nazareth. To what do you attribute this?

The most important reason is that every Sunday in church a Jesus is preached who was born of a virgin and is said to be true God, but at the same time also truly human and without sin. In this way Jesus becomes part of a fairy-tale world which we cannot enter because of our universal awareness of what is the truth. Therefore on the one hand fewer and fewer people go to church , while on the other hand there is undiminished interest in who Jesus really was. In this way, with its preaching, which is orientated on past creeds, the church has provoked new questions about Jesus.

That is a clear criticism of the church. But is there not also here a failure of theology, which should provide all those involved in the church with good arguments?

Protestant theology is tied to its confession. It is bound by confessional documents including creeds from the time of the early church. Even a critical systematic theologian like Gerhard Ebeling, who almost more than anyone else has investigated the historical Jesus, shies off for example the issue of the sinlessness of Jesus by not putting it in question, but affirming it undiminished and giving an extended justification of it. This is quite incredible to anyone making a historical investigation. If Jesus was really human, how could he have been without sin, especially as he had himself been baptized by John the Baptist 'for the forgiveness of sins'? Even Ebeling, along with many other critical systematic theologians, continues to settle for the christology of the early church and simply dodges history. I think that the presupposition that Jesus was sinless and the fact that this is still asserted is a scandal.

So are you claiming that Protestant theology at the German universities is in the grip of the churches?

Yes, for the most part theology is definitely a church discipline. That was already the case in the last century and was reinforced in our century by Karl Barth's *Church Dogmatics*. By contrast, I think that I am not helping my church if I emphasize the ecclesiastical nature of theology. For that prevents me from seeking the truth. A science of Christian faith is no more Christian than the science of criminology is criminal. Like all other disciplines, theology seeks the truth. It cannot presuppose any results.

To what do you attribute the fact that theologians doing academic work put it at the service of the church as they do?

There is a close link between theological faculties and the church. Most of my colleagues sit on church bodies and indeed are pleased to be appointed to them. Many theological professors have even been ordained subsequently. That really goes against the Protestant understanding of ordination, which is closely bound up with the pastorate. To be ordained subsequently indicates a Catholic way of thinking which in some way seeks additional certainties and starts from a two-class society: clergy on the one hand and laity on the other.

Is there also a psychological side to this development?

That may be. Perhaps there is also an anxiety about not possessing the truth. Perhaps that is why many seek the blessing of the church later. But that puts a burden on theology. For any dispute between the church and truth will then rapidly be decided in favour of the church. However, a critical theology must say that in cases of conflict the truth has precedence over the church.

The newly awakened interest in the person of Jesus probably also has something to do with the Qumran discoveries. How seriously do you take the publications of some critics who, starting from these discoveries, claim that Christianity merely constructed the uniqueness of Jesus and used force to impose it? In reality was Jesus merely the member of a Jewish sect?

This view is untenable. It comes to grief on the texts if they are read critically. It emerges from the texts that Jesus was initially a disciple of John the Baptist. He had himself baptized by John. A further judgment based on facts is that he then parted company with John, founded his own movement and called disciples. Anything else is sheer nonsense.

Let's go on to your criticism. In your new book you call Paul 'the first heretic'. But he is generally regarded as the most important apostle, evangelist and theologian of Christianity. What do you mean by calling him a heretic?

By that I understand that Paul was the first person to be called a heretic, i.e. a wicked man to be repudiated, by another Christian group. In fact the community in Jerusalem introduced the term heretic into Christianity. It was then an irony of history that a century later offshoots of this community were called heretics.

The majority of New Testament scholars are increasingly agreed that historically speaking Paul was the first heretic. How a Christian group departed radically from Paul, indeed even attacked him and cast him out, can be reconstructed clearly. This process was repeated in many places in primitive Christianity, so that we can say that the phenomenon of demarcation, of vilification, of rejection, of fighting with one another, was much more widespread in the first two centuries, during which the New Testament came into being, than is generally assumed.

Nevertheless a doctrinal view prevailed.

Yes, but which? Certainly not Paul's, since his theology was changed by others in various ways. Among other things, after his death even letters were forged in his name. This is the way in which the New Testament canon was gradually formed.

Early Christian theology was stamped above all by the apologetic conflict with Gnosticism, which was repudiated as false teaching. That is true to the present day. Against the background of your historical-critical reflections would Gnosticism have to be rehabilitated today?

Let me give an example: the resurrection of Jesus or the resurrection of the faithful. The church which proved victorious in the theological controversies at the end of the second century asserted and confessed in the Creed the resurrection of the flesh. Today we confess the resurrection of the dead, but formerly people spoke of the resurrection of the flesh. The groups which established the New Testament in fact began from a fleshly resurrection of Jesus. How do we deal with that today? We can either continue to assert it and thus lose all credibility, or we have to understand and formulate the Christian hope in quite a different way. Here the Gnostic answer could help, since it takes the resurrection as a symbol for something firm, which cannot be stated. At this point I regard an investigation of the Gnostic statements about resurrection as indispensable, because the Gnostics were the only theologians of the early period who had ideas on this point and chose formulations which are credible.

One of the most important criticisms of Gnosticism was its dualism, the falling apart of this world and the beyond, and the way in which human beings perfected themselves and became divine beings. Surely a rehabilitation of this idea would be going too far, because among other things it would do away with the Reformation belief in justification?

The concept of Gnosticism is highly controversial. It is not clear whether it means an independent movement or a structure within the Christian religion. I do not want to claim that the church fathers got everything wrong. However, on the threshold of the third millennium we need to accept the challenges of our time, using all the documents inside and outside the Bible. For the question of creation I think the early church's answer absolutely necessary. Here dualism is harmful and takes us away from responsibility for the earth.

Here among other things the tension between religion and science, myth and rationality becomes clear. You resolve this tension almost completely in favour of rationality. But in the course of the discussion on postmodernity it has proved how abidingly relevant myths are for us human beings. Doesn't your exegesis neglect this insight?

That is a charge which is frequently levelled at me, but I don't find it relevant. Certainly I make use of historical criticism. Who would claim that that is unnecessary? However, I would only be a rationalist if I explained the Easter faith, intellectually, as an 'interpretation', to use Rudolf Bultmann's term. But through my historical work I come to put a strong emphasis on the emotional side of the origin of the Easter faith. I even criticize a Protestant theology which is prejudiced about visions.

However, I am convinced that the tomb was full and that Jesus' body decayed. For human beings die, and must come to terms with certain realities. Here it is simply a matter of a sober contemplation which talks honestly about certain things, including those that are inconvenient. But that is far from being rationalism.

Among other things, critics accuse you of choosing a false start-ing point for your exegetical work. Instead of lovingly trying to understand what the texts are seeking to say on the basis of tradition, you subject everything to modern scientific thought. Klaus Berger calls this a 'subtle cultural imperialism which does not do justice to the Bible's culture of perception'. Does this charge apply to you?

This criticism was directed against my book on the resurrection. I can only say that I was concerned with quite a different question. I am interested in what really happened at Easter. In answering this question I am not at all helped by a reference to the Bible's culture of perception. The question of the facts is of prime importance, since on the one hand the Bible says that the tomb was empty and on the other, for example the Gospel according to Matthew knows a Jewish version, that the tomb was not at all empty, but that the disciples stole the body. Therefore the question of historical truth is unavoidable.

Furthermore, a responsible exegete and historian must reconstruct past history to get closer to what actually happened. Conclusions are then to be drawn from this reconstruction of past history, which is superior to that of the Bible.

Can you give a concrete example?

Let's take the Gospel according to Mark and what is said there about the Jews. Mark alone reports three times that Jesus goes to Jerusalem to be put to death by the Jewish authorities. If we take into account the Bible's culture of perception here, we can quite obviously detect anti-Jewish thought. That can also be demonstrated from other biblical passages. I don't see how we can deal appropriately with these statements without questioning and reconstruction.

Does that mean that in your view in the past two thousand years the preaching of the church has been, if not false, at least partially wrong?

'Partially wrong' is not a very friendly way of putting it. First of all I am speaking as a scholar. I reconstruct history and write books about it. I do not reflect on the significance of that for the church. However, there is no disputing the fact that in some questions things can come out very badly. Let's take the relationship of the church to the Jews as an example. That is why I prefer to discuss present-day questions and not so much whether the past was partially right or wrong. What matters is what is right today.

Nevertheless, we cannot ignore our origin and our heritage. We stand in certain continuities which shape our present. Your scholarly researches necessarily have effects on the church and its preaching.

Yes, but I am concerned above all about the future. We are now entering the third millennium and must reflect on the role that the church and the Christian tradition are to have in the future. I am writing for this future. Unless we remain open to the future, neither academic theology in the colleges nor the church in society have a perspective. In that case scholarship allies itself with unbelief and the church with barbarism, as Schleiermacher put it.

What changes do you think are most urgently necessary for the church?

Above all the church must put itself in a relationship to Jesus of Nazareth as he is suggested by historical reconstruction, and not to the risen Lord. The latter is already an interpretation of the first Christians. Following Rudolf Bultmann, in New Testament theology hitherto a sharp distinction has been drawn between Jesus and Christ: according to this, the Jew Jesus belongs to the presuppositions of Christian religion, but real Christianity begins only with the proclamation of Christ. That was a construction with which people were happy to live since with it they could integrate all of church preaching and leave Jesus out as a 'hard lump'. But in my view that no longer works. Jesus was the first Christian. That should have consequences for the church and also for my personal faith.

But would that mean that even the Creed had to be reformulated?

Yes indeed. The Apostles' Creed that we recite every Sunday says: born of the Virgin Mary, crucified under Pontius Pilate, suffered and was buried, and so on. The whole Jesus is missing from these formulations: his life, his person, his preaching. All that must be brought much more into the foreground. Moreover with all due respect I regard the whole christology of the early church as obsolete. It is an element of the tradition which no longer has any significance for our preaching today or for our life generally.

On these presuppositions, is christology possible at all?

It would probably be better to say Jesuology, but the name doesn't matter. The important thing is to reconstruct Jesus, his person and the message that he brought, in an understandable way. So my future works will be concerned to make progress here. A separation between Jesus and Christ is quite possible. The resurrection is not a historical event. To see this simply calls for intellectual honesty. In this connection we can remember the well-known saying, 'Jesus expected the kingdom of God and the church came.' That cannot be evaded by saying that Jesus and Christ cannot be separated.

How then, in your view, can the resurrection be interpreted?

Perhaps here, too, the Gnostics help us. At one point the Gospel of Philip sensibly states: those who say that Jesus died and rose are wrong. Rather it should be said, he rose and died. Here the resurrection is a symbol for something firm. That could also apply to a religious experience which can be had in this life and not first in the other world. The statement could be: those who have recognized God here, and thus also themselves, those who have penetrated to what is firm, have overcome death. When I personally speak about resurrection I am talking about this experience of what is absolute and firm. And I believe that in this way one can also build a way for modern contemporaries to adopt the substance of Christianity.

Is that also a rejection of any form of eschatology?

I think that it is extremely difficult to make statements about the last things. To this degree traditional eschatology which counts on a temporal return of Jesus is quite unbelievable for me, and I can't go along with it. Quite apart from that, the first Christians saw themselves as the only and last Christians. For Jesus was to come again in their lifetime. However, that did not happen. The expectation of the end proved to be an error. And I do not know how one can go on living with that after two thousand years.

Many Christians have done so down the centuries.

Yes, but there have always been honest people who have seen through it. A colleague whose name I do not want to mention once told a story about Rudolf Bultmann: whenever he had students at his home he asked them individually to state clearly whether they thought that Jesus would return from heaven. In asking this he wanted to force them to be honest and not simply to maintain a tradition. I think that that is the only thing that one can do in this question: to be honest and become a bit more modest.

Closely connected with this is the question of redemption. In the preaching of the church, Jesus as the Christ was always the Redeemer who frees human beings from their sins. If we follow your line, this idea too must be shelved. How then would you describe Jesus?

As a human being. In the preaching of Jesus there is a clear tendency to interpret the tradition in the light of love and in favour of human beings. Here he is completely on the ground of the tradition of Israel and was therefore also moved by the hope that the kingdom of God would dawn in the immediate future. He had a tense expectation of the end.

If we consider Jesus as a human being we must grant that he was neither sinless nor without error. He evidently expected something that did not happen. But that does not mean that we can't learn a great deal from him: from his parables, from the beatitudes he spoke over the poor, or the fact that God accepts the godless. This message of Jesus can speak to people and move them so that it becomes the foundation of their lives.

But surely this would remove the transcendent dimension of Christian faith, what is traditionally described by the figure of heaven?

What does heaven mean here? The dimension which breaks open the realm of facts can be described in various terms; for example one can speak of the ground of being. I think that our life points to something else, and here I recall Troeltsch, who said, 'The beyond is the force in this life.' However, we must learn to express this hope anew.

Have you taken into account the fact that many people will simply regard your ideas as an attack on Christianity?

I think it nonsensical that, for example, schoolchildren should be introduced to physics or chemistry but should remain illiterate in the religious sphere. Nevertheless the illiteracy which is in fact present among wide circles of the German population need not lead to resignation in respect of early Christianity. For the consequence can only be to regard education about this, too, as a task and to introduce it into churches and schools.

With your approach you question many ideas handed down by the church. Have you ever been put under pressure by church officials?

In a major national newspaper my colleague Klaus Berger from Heidelberg has considered disciplinary proceedings against me. This is not a possibility because I am not ordained. I am merely a civil servant. Otherwise I don't feel under pressure in any way. On the other hand some pastors have written to me saying that for similar views they have been forced by the church to give up their opinions or withdraw books from circulation. Evidently proceedings are taken against dissidents within the church. But it is schizophrenia to leave the confessions as they are and to ordain pastors to something which they can no longer believe which they are then to preach as the Word of God. The hypocrisy could hardly be greater!*

Do you yourself still take your stand on scripture and confession?

No – for reasons of conscience. For example, I cannot take my stand on the Apostles' Creed, since the Virgin Birth stated there demonstrably did not take place. Nor can I take my stand on scripture, since the Bible is not the Word of God but a work of the catholic church of the second century. Unfortunately we heard little of this human side even in 1992, 'The Year of the Bible'.

*As a result of this criticism, I have since been dismissed from the Board of the Protestant Federation of the Churches of Lower Saxony, responsible for examining theological students, to which traditionally every theological professor there belongs.

Problems and Methods

A split consciousness in dealing with the Bible

For the Christian churches, present and past, the Bible is Holy Scripture. The vast majority of Christians read the Bible in the literal sense as the inspired Word of God, a view which was universal up to the Enlightenment.

Nevertheless, for scholarly theology the scriptural principle presupposed here has been shelved once for all as a result of the disintegration of the dogma of inspiration.

Wolfhart Pannenberg's classic 1962 article on 'The Crisis of the Scripture Principle' explains what has happened. Martin Luther, Pannenberg points out, engaged in combat with the papal magisterium by referring to the exegetically clear literal sense of scripture, convinced that his own exegetical results were *identical* with the '"essential content" of scripture, as it is concentrated in the person and history of Jesus Christ and unfolded in the dogmas of the church' (1970: 5). His certainty was the basis for his hermeneutical principle that scripture was clear or self-evident. 'The doctrine of the clarity of Scripture necessarily led to the demand that each theological statement should be based on the historical-critical exposition of Scripture' (6). Nevertheless, historical biblical criticism conjured up the fundamental crisis with which we are confronted today. Whereas for Luther the literal sense of the scriptures was still identical with its historical content, today the two have drifted apart: 'The picture of Jesus and his history which the various New Testament authors give us cannot ... be regarded as identical with the actual course of events ... For us ... it is impossible to overlook the historical distance between any theology possible today and the primitive Christian period. This distance has become the source of our most vexing theological problems' (6). In other words, the gulf between historical fact and its alleged meaning, between history and proclamation, between the actual history of Jesus and the variegated picture of his history in the New Testament, makes it impossible to continue to argue seriously that the writings of the New Testament are inspired, or even to identify the Word of God with Holy Scripture.

So far these assured insights have made little impact on a naive fundamentalist reading. Rather, the view prevails almost universally today that as I read Holy Scripture God is addressing me, and that this form of address is the same as the form of address to those who received the biblical testimonies or those to whom these testimonies were given.

However, a number of presuppositions are indispensable for such a construction. First, that the present biblical canon was established by God himself. Secondly, that the authors who speak or write in it are doing so on orders from God. Thirdly, that they are addressing not only their contemporaries but also those who were later to read their writings or words. As I have already remarked, this implies that the meaning or the content of the message then and now is identical. What was said or written then, applies equally today. So Luther could 'identify his own doctrine with the content of the biblical writings, literally understood' (Pannenberg 1970: 6).

Nowadays, this assumption and the scriptural principle associated with it can only be termed naive, even if in the Luther anniversary year 1996 the Reformer's heritage is formally conjured up and it is impressed on us how far Luther is ahead of us (cf. Hirscher 1996). For there is no mistaking the enormously deep gulf of history that has opened up between then and now. The historical distance between the time of early Christianity and the present-day church caused a critical whirlpool which inexorably drags favourite customary beliefs down with it into the depths. This happens because the historical-critical investigation of the Bible which has now been carried on for 250 years (cf. Reventlow 1985; Hirsch 1964; for the Old Testament,

Smend 1991; for the New Testament, Kümmel 1970, 1973), completely did away with the previous picture of the Bible and taught us to understand every single verse of it as a human word. However, the results of this investigation have been communicated to the general public only sparingly – if at all. The impression that Christoph Türcke has gained of theology as practised today is worth reporting. This critic of so-called academic theology, who is ignored by the theological guild, writes: 'God is translated into the most elaborate scholarly terms – but 1. always on the simple presupposition that he exists and has given a meaning and purpose to history, and 2. always with the intent of confirming this simple presupposition as the ultimate wisdom' (Türcke 1992: 136). He continues:

> The reflection on the creed that takes place as scholars go through it is a cover-up of its naivety laundered by all the waters of the Enlightenment. The creed reflected on in this way is two things at the same time: it is both naive and strained. This duality is the signature of modern theology. Like a chameleon it can change colour, indignantly reject the charge of naivety with reference to its scientific character, and the charge that its academic approach is dissecting the substance of faith with reference to its roots in the creed – and thus perform the task of a double mimicry: of the standards of academic discussion *and* the simple faith of the worshipping community (Türcke 1992: 136f.).

Türcke's diagnosis that present-day theology has a split consciousness may well be right. For on the one hand this theology is concerned to link up with the tradition of the councils of the early church and its doctrinal decisions, and for example defends the Apostles' Creed at any price. On the other hand, in biblical exegesis it is indebted to its liberal heritage and thus to the historical-critical method. But for quite some time the results of historical research have been either (a) bent, (b) relativized, (c) tamed, or (d) generally put in question in a wider framework with obscure methods.

(a) The results of historical research are bent when, for

example, the false attribution of New Testament writings is played down and reference is made to their being based on an undeveloped awareness of intellectual property and of the individuality of the author. II Thessalonians is an example which tells against such a general theory; it explicitly takes a stand against a forgery (II Thess. 2.2) and yet is itself a forgery (for the problem see Lüdemann 1996: 108–20).

(b) The results of historical research are relativized where, for example, it is said that even if it could be proved beyond doubt that the tomb of Jesus was not empty at Easter, but full, this would have no significance for faith in the risen Christ (thus e.g. Lindemann 1994). This expedient is unsatisfactory because it completely twists the traditional content of the word 'resurrection'. One can apply the test, 'Can anyone who supports Lindemann's position still pray to Christ?' I think not.

(c) The results of historical criticism are tamed where it is said that they must not be made absolute (thus Bishop Horst Hirschler in a lecture given on 24 June 1996 within the framework of the Bonn Theological Conversations of the Protestant Sections of the Christian Democratic Union and the Christian Social Union; cf. *idea* 78, 1996). Historical criticism is valid universally or not at all. To this degree it must absolutize itself and its results. However, that does not mean that it claims to be able to grasp the whole of reality.

(d) The results of historical research have been vigorously questioned e.g. by Carsten P. Thiede and Matthew d'Ancona (1995), on the basis of a redating of the New Testament Gospels and the associated thesis that these were composed by eyewitnesses. Werner Harenberg (1996) has impressively shown that here the public is being grossly deceived.

The revised Luther Bible and its picture of Holy Scripture

One example of the way in which the Bible is being introduced and communicated to the Protestant church public in Germany is the preface to the Revised Luther Bible of 1984 by Bishop

Eduard Lohse, the then President of the Council of the Protestant Church in Germany and the German Bible Society (I am quoting from the 1985 edition; the preface is no longer printed in editions after 1989). The 'Preface on Holy Scripture' states:

> The Bible seeks to bring to all men and women the good news of God's mercy ... The earliest witnesses of the Old Testament go back to the time when Israel was going from the wilderness into the promised land. The history of this people is told, the message of its prophets is proclaimed, and the praise to God in the psalms is sung.
>
> The majority of the writings of the New Testament were written down in the second half of the first century after Christ: first the letters of the apostle Paul, then the reports of Jesus' activity, his suffering, death and resurrection; finally, in addition, some writings were composed at the beginning of the second century.
>
> Each biblical writing speaks to a particular historical situation. It addresses people who know anxieties and joys, sorrow and happiness, and tells them that God's Word seeks to comfort them and raise them up, govern and direct their lives. The biblical witnesses hand on what they have experienced: God's Word is true and can be relied upon. What was true yesterday is also true today, tomorrow and for ever. This testimony has been handed down from one generation to the next. No other book has been translated into as many languages as the Bible. No other work is read among so many peoples as it is.
>
> Martin Luther translated the whole of the New Testament into German on the Wartburg within eighty days. The printed edition appeared in September 1522, and all the writings of the Old Testament had been translated by 1534. Luther's Bible has stamped the German language to the present day. It was and is of incomparable power, which is at work in the community and also proves itself in personal Bible reading ...

Just as the Reformation took its beginning from listening to the biblical message, so too in the future the Luther Bible will be a unifying bond for German-speaking Protestant Christianity.

Martin Luther constantly stressed that the Bible contains a treasure of wisdom that we can never exhaust, and that we can never come to an end in understanding. Immediately before his death he still noted: 'Let no one think that he has tasted Holy Scripture enough, unless he has led churches with the prophets for a hundred years.' Some biblical sayings only disclose themselves after one has pondered on them for a long time. That does not mean that the Bible is 'obscure'. The message of the merciful and newly-creating love of God shines as brightly and clearly from it as the sun. Those who open this book and allow it to speak to them will experience even today what trust there is in life and death, and can grate-fully confess with our fathers and mothers, 'The word of our God abides for ever' (Isa. 40.8).

This preface combines the results of historical criticism of the Bible and key theological formulations. Accordingly, in the translation which follows, key statements of the Bible are printed in bold type, and at the end a chronological survey is given of the presumed time of composition of the biblical books along with the secular dates presupposed in it. In addition, it should be noted that in the translation account is taken of the most recent text-critical evidence: thus for example Mark 16.9–20 is explicitly indicated as a conclusion added to the Gospel of Mark only later.

Thus the Luther Bible in the revised version of 1984 with its preface and appendices is an example of the present-day position and use of the Bible within the German Protestant church, a church which is stamped by biblical criticism, and whose official representatives on many occasions boast to their Roman Catholic counterparts of their Protestant freedom.

However, it should be pointed out that the results of histori-cal criticism are not noted consistently in the revised Luther

Bible. I shall now discuss three points which cry out for contradiction.

The proof from prophecy

In the preface, an Old Testament saying is cited for something believed by all Christians. In the translation of the Old Testament which follows, among others those passages are printed in bold which Christianity has for centuries regarded as prophecies of the coming of Jesus and which are recited every year at Christmas (Isa. 7.10–14; 9.1–6; 11.1–9; Micah 5.1–4a; II Sam.7.4–6, 12–14a) or Good Friday worship (Isa. 53.4–5). But hasn't historical criticism of the Bible shown universally and once for all that those passages of the Old Testament which are cited by the Christian church as prophecies of the coming of Christ are nothing of the kind? Isn't it terrible that every Christmas this farce is enacted with the Old Testament before unsuspecting listeners who go to church only once a year? What distinguishes the present-day church in its misuse of the Old Testament from those Christian theologians of the second century whom Friedrich Nietzsche once severely criticized as follows?

> What can be expected from the effects of a religion which, during the centuries when it was being finally established, enacted that huge philological farce concerning the Old Testament? I refer to that attempt to tear the Old Testament from the hands of the Jews under the pretext that it contained only Christian doctrines and *belonged* to the Christians as the *true* people of Israel, while the Jews had merely arrogated it to themselves without authority. This was followed by a mania of would-be interpretation and falsification, which could not under any circumstances have been allied with a good conscience. However strongly Jewish savants protested, it was everywhere sedulously asserted that the Old Testament alluded everywhere to Christ, and nothing but Christ, more especially His cross, and thus wherever reference was made to wood, a rod, a ladder, a twig, a tree, a willow, or a staff, such

a reference could not but be a prophecy relating to the wood of the Cross; even the setting up of the Unicorn and the Bronze Serpent, even Moses stretching forth his hands in prayer, yes, the very spits on which the Easter lambs were roasted: all these were allusions to the cross, and, as it were, pointers ot it. Did anyone who kept on asserting these things ever *believe* in them? (*The Dawn of Day* I, 84: Nietzsche 1911).

Example 1: Isa. 7.14

To the present day Isa. 7.14 is seen as a mysterious prophecy of the birth of Jesus. This interpretation goes back to the author of the Gospel of Matthew, who in the framework of the story of the announcement of the birth of Jesus writes:

> All this took place to fulfil what the Lord had spoken by the prophet: 'Behold, a virgin (*parthenos*) shall conceive and bear a son, and his name shall be called Emmanuel (which means, God with us)' (Matt. 1.22f.).

This saying is a so-called 'reflective' or 'fulfilment quotation'. The First Evangelist is concerned to show that certain Old Testament promises were fulfilled in Jesus.

However, the interpretation that in 7.14 Isaiah prophesied the birth of *Jesus* is arbitrary and untenable. This is clear from a look at the context and the historical background of the saying cited. In 733 BCE a group of Syro-Palestinian states allied to offer common resistance to the threat posed by the expansionist policy of the Assyrian king Tiglath-pileser III (745–727 BCE). When King Ahaz of Judah refused to join their coalition, Rezin of Damascus (Syria) and Pekah of Israel (Ephraim) advanced on Jerusalem, to overthrow the Davidic dynasty and replace it with a king who would fall in with their plans (Isa. 7.1–6; II Kings 16.5). Ahaz, who evidently did not feel up to coping with the assailants, thereupon looked round for a more powerful ally and finally contemplated asking Tiglath-pileser III himself for help against Rezin and Pekah (cf.

II Kings 16.7) and submitting to him voluntarily. But this would have been tantamount to an acknowledgment of the Assyrian state deities and thus would have represented a breach of loyalty to Yahweh (for the name Yahweh see 34 below).

In this situation the prophet Isaiah turns to Ahaz and calls on him to keep calm, trusting in Yahweh's help (Isa. 7.4, 7–9). When this invitation bears no fruit and Ahaz maintains his resolve to seek help from the Assyrian great power, Isaiah meets the king a second time and offers him a sign in Yahweh's name (Isa. 7.11). But Ahaz rejects this offer (Isa. 7.12), whereupon Isaiah says to him:

> 13 And he said, 'Hear then, house of David! Is it too little for you to weary men, that you weary my God also? 14a Therefore the Lord himself will give you a sign. 14b Behold, a young woman ('*alma*) is pregnant and will bear a son, and shall call his name Immanuel (= God with us). 15 [He shall eat curds and honey when he knows how to refuse the evil and choose the good.] 16a For before the child knows how to refuse the evil and choose the good, 16b the land before whose two kings you are in dread will be deserted. 17a Yahweh will bring upon you and upon your people and upon your father's house such days as have not come since the day that Ephraim departed from Judah 17b [the king of Assyria].'

Scholars have long puzzled over the meaning of these words. Essentially three different answers to the question who is meant by the 'son' can be distinguished (for what follows see Kilian 1983, 15–26): (a) a messianic figure; (b) Hezekiah, the son of Ahaz; (c) a son of Isaiah (cf. Isa. 7.3; 8.1–4). However, none of these interpretations can be sustained:

(a) The messianic understanding which finds here the prophecy of the birth of an eschatological king of salvation is vitiated by the fact that the overall context of the section is one of *disaster* (see below).

(b) The assumption that the 'son' is a reference to the prince

Hezekiah cannot be sustained on chronological grounds. As emerges from II Kings 16.2 and 18.2, Hezekiah ascended the throne at the age of twenty-five, after his father had ruled for sixteen years (as sole ruler). Accordingly in 733 BCE Hezekiah was already nine years old.

(c) Shear-yashub and Spoil speeds-Prey hastens are explicitly said to be sons of Isaiah in the immediate context of Isa. 7.14 (cf. 7.3; 8.3). Thus it is improbable that Isaiah had yet another son in addition to these two during the Syro-Ephraimite war.

As the three interpretations mentioned above are ruled out, the two following alternatives remain, depending on whether one regards the conclusion of Isa. 7.16b as original or secondary (the question whether vv. 15 and 17b are primary or not can be left out of account here):

If the conclusion of v.16b is *original*, then a collective interpretation of Immanuel seems likely. In that case the meaning of Isa. 7.14–17 can be formulated as follows: the threat posed by the alliance against Judah will indeed cease so soon that women who are now pregnant can gratefully call their children 'Immanuel'. But the consequence of the king's unbelief is that the life of these children born in an apparently happy hour will take a course which contrasts sharply with their saving names. For before they can distinguish between good and evil, conditions will predominate comparable only with the collapse of the kingdom after Solomon's death (thus Kaiser 1972: 100f.).

Kaiser 1983 advances the view that Isa. 7.10–14a, 17 contains the basic stratum (which is not Isaianic) of Isa. 7.10–17. This has later been extended by a 'messianic revision with an eschatology of salvation (116) comprising vv.14b–16b (up to 'be forsaken', cf. 151–70). For the doubtful nature of this thesis see the summary in Kilian 1983, 13f.

If the conclusion of v.16b is *secondary*, then the land of *Judah* will be forsaken and there is no promise of salvation in vv.14–17. In this case we can even ask whether v.14b cannot be understood to mean that people 'will soon utter "Immanuel" as a cry for *help*, to which the king is deaf ... in its traditional sense as an expression of *trust*' (Lescow 1967: 176; cf. 180).

The conclusion to be drawn is that whatever decision one arrives at in terms of literary criticism, it is clear that the context of Isa. 7.14 in the view of the prophet calls for an event which takes place at least during the lifetime of Ahaz. That rules out a *christological* interpretation of Isa. 7.14. Such an interpretation is also absurd because the First Evangelist regards Jesus as the son of a virgin, and for this refers to the Greek translation of the Old Testament. The Hebrew original does not have 'virgin' at all but 'young woman'. The Jews have always pointed this out and rightly objected to the christological interpretation of the Gospel of Matthew.

We have to imagine the development in the following terms. The early Christians took over the idea of a virgin birth of the Messiah from the Hellenistic Jewish environment (cf. Koester 1990: 306f.), and Matthew then 'discovered' it in the Greek translation of the Old Testament (in addition to Matt. 1.22, cf. also Luke 2.27).

Hermann Samuel Reimarus, to whose significance for biblical exegesis I shall return later (see below, 51f.), passed a devastating judgment on the arbitrary interpretation of Isa. 7.14.

> The prophet Isaiah is regarded as the prime evangelist, and no passage is more strongly pressed by the Messiah's advent in the flesh than the one which Matthew also cites: 'Behold, a virgin will become pregnant and will bear a son whose name she will call Immanuel.' Isaiah presented this son to king Ahaz as a sign and an assurance that very soon indeed he would have nothing more to fear from the kings in Israel and Damascus who had again advanced on Jerusalem. 'For before this boy knows how to reject evil and to choose good, the land for which you are afraid will be abandoned by its two kings.' Here it is indeed clear enough that this cannot refer to the birth of a boy who is to come into the world only 700 years later. For the lands of Israel and Damascus were to be forsaken before the boy had learned to reject evil and do

good. That does not mean more than 700 years. And what is more natural than that a sign which was given as an assurance for the future should have preceded the future? How could the unbelieving, idolatrous king be convinced of the certainty of what was so imminent for him by a far remoter miracle of which he did not know and in which he did not believe? The Jews legitimately insist on this, and Christian interpreters torture themselves in vain, and cannot in any way give a satisfactory answer (1972a: 735f.).

Example 2: Isa. 52.13–53.12

Down to the present day this text has been understood as a prophecy of the passion of Jesus. However, in this case, too, a short glance at its origin and its historical context makes a christological interpretation impossible.

The book of Isaiah is not a unitary literary structure but a collection of prophetic texts which has come into being only in the course of centuries. Only in the first complex of the book (chs.1–39) does the prophet Isaiah (second half of the eighth century BCE) speak and act; by contrast the second part (chs.40–55) contains the message of an unknown prophet of the time of the exile whom scholars have come to refer to as Deutero-Isaiah (Second Isaiah). The main theme of this work is the message that Yahweh will bring those who have been deported back from Babylonia to their homeland. The nucleus of the third part (chs.56–66) is formed by the proclamation of another unknown prophet who is called Trito-Isaiah (Third Isaiah) and was probably active in Palestine around 530 BCE.

The so-called 'Servant Songs' (Isa. 42.1–4 [–9]; 49.1–6 [–13]; 50. 4–9 [–11]; 52.13–53.12) stand out from the context of the second complex as an independent and coherent stratum. The conclusion and climax is formed by the fourth song, in which two statements by Yahweh (52.13–15; 53.11b–12) frame the confession of a group which speaks in the first person plural:

> 52.13 Behold, my servant shall prosper, he shall be exalted and lifted up, and shall be very high. 14 As many were

astonished at him – his appearance was so marred, beyond human semblance, and his form beyond that of the sons of men – 15 so shall he startle many nations; kings shall shut their mouths because of him; for that which has not been told them they shall see, and that which they have not heard they shall understand.

53.1 Who has believed what we have heard? And to whom has the arm of Yahweh been revealed? 2 For he grew up before him like a young plant, and like a root out of dry ground; he had no form or comeliness that we should look at him, and no beauty that we should desire him. 3 He was despised and rejected by men; a man of sorrows, and acquainted with grief; and as one from whom men hide their faces he was despised, and we esteemed him not. 4 Surely he has borne our griefs and carried our sorrows; yet we esteemed him stricken, smitten by God, and afflicted. 5 But he was wounded for our transgressions, he was bruised for our iniquities; upon him was the chastisement that made us whole, and with his stripes we are healed. 6 All we like sheep have gone astray; we have turned every one to his own way; and Yahweh has laid on him the iniquity of us all. 7 He was oppressed, and he was afflicted, yet he opened not his mouth; like a lamb that is led to the slaughter, and like a sheep that before its shearers is dumb, so he opened not his mouth. 8 By oppression and judgment he was taken away; and as for his generation, who considered that he was cut off out of the land of the living, stricken for the transgression of my people? 9 And they made his grave with the godless and the wicked [M with the rich] in his death, although he had done no violence and there was no deceit in his mouth. 10 Yet it was the will of the Lord to bruise him; he has put him to grief; when he makes himself an offering for sin, he shall see his offspring, he shall prolong his days; the will of Yahweh shall prosper in his hand; 11 he shall see the fruit of the travail of his soul and be satisfied.

By his knowledge shall the righteous one, my servant, make many to be accounted righteous; and he shall bear their iniquities. 12 Therefore I will divide him a portion with the great, and he shall divide the spoil with the strong; because he poured out his soul to death, and was numbered with the transgressors; yet he bore the sin of many, and made intercession for the transgressors.

This text, which is still recited in worship every Good Friday, is presented to church people as a prophecy of Jesus' passion. By contrast, that interpretation no longer plays any role in modern exegesis. Nevertheless there is still a dispute over whom Deutero-Isaiah in fact meant by the servant of Yahweh and whether he is looking back to him, expecting him or understanding him as a contemporary.

Three different interpretations can be distinguished: (a) collective, (b) individual prophetic, and (c) individual royal. I shall give the most important arguments for and against these interpretations as briefly as possible (cf. Koch 1983: 143–7).

(a) The advocates of the collective interpretation who see the servant of God as the actual or the real Israel or an essential part of it (the exilic community) point out that in other passages of the book of Deutero-Isaiah Israel is explicitly called 'servant' (cf. 41.8; 44.1f., 21; in 49.3 'Israel' is a later addition). However, the fact that the servant is given a clear action to perform to Israel with the charge 'to raise up the tribes of Jacob and to restore the preserved of Israel' (49.6), in other words to liberate those who have been deported from the Babylonian exile, tells against this interpretation.

(b) The assumption that a prophetic figure, possibly Deutero-Isaiah himself, is concealed behind the servant is based on the statements that the islands are waiting for his 'instruction' (42.4), that Yahweh has given him 'a mouth like a sharp sword' (49.2), and that he makes a covenant like Moses, who was regarded as a prophet in the exilic period (42.6). However, it suffers from the fact that the servant does not have any features which are characteristic only of a prophet and in particular does not carry out the service of a messenger on behalf of Yahweh.

(c) The individual-royal interpretation is supported by the

courtly presentation of the servant by Yahweh (42.1; 52.13–15)
and parallel motives from the royal ideology (being called in his
mother's womb; being addressed as the 'chosen servant' whom
God takes by the hand; the combination of the bestowal of the
spirit, the pronouncement of justice and providing care); against
it is the fact that the servant is nowhere designated 'king' and
has no warlike features.

So it is impossible to decide with certainty who the servant of
Yahweh is. But at the same time, regardless of whether one has
a preference for one of the three possibilities or leaves the
question open, it is clear that the songs must be seen and
interpreted in their historical context and that like the whole
proclamation of Deutero-Isaiah, they presuppose the current
situation of the prophet as determined by the exile and have
been pronounced against that background.

Thus no matter whom Deutero-Isaiah meant by the servant,
he was certainly not thinking of *Jesus* and the events which
Christians later understood as a fulfilment of his words. That
already emerges from the fact that Jesus himself did not regard
any of the main tasks of the servant of God as his own, 'namely
to liberate the deported Israelites and bring them back to
Palestine, and to found a new state and a new cult' (Koch 1983:
146).

It is often argued against this that the prophecy fulfilled itself
in a different way from what was expected, or that its real
meaning only became clear in the light of the fulfilment. Anyone
who argues in this way not only evacuates the term 'prophecy'
of its accepted meaning of a prediction of a future event, but
also lays claim to the text in a way contrary to the original
intention of the author.

In the period before the Enlightenment it was possible to deal
with the Old Testament in this way with a good conscience.
Martin Luther's interpretation of Scripture still belongs in this
period. Today, by contrast, such a use of the Old Testament is
excluded on the grounds that *we know better* (cf. Gunneweg
1978).

The notion of the Bible as Word of God

Both the Old Testament and the New Testament or its elements
are explicitly regarded as the Word of God in the preface of the
revised Luther Bible, and both are regarded as Holy Scripture.
Certainly a modern systematic theologian can still write that it
is wrong to say that 'Holy Scripture *contains* the Word of God
in human discourse' (Slenczka 1991: 59), but *is* not the Word of
God, since with that 'view, spirit and letters in Holy Scripture
are separated' (ibid.). Rather, '*The Holy Scripture of the Old
and New Testament is the Word of the Triune God, in which he
makes himself known, through which he is present, speaks and
acts*' (38). But on the whole this view no longer finds assent in
Protestant academic theology and is more in keeping with
Roman Catholic thought, according to which, 'The Holy
Scriptures contain the Word of God and, because they are
inspired, they are truly the Word of God' (Lohfink 1967: 17
n.9; *Catechism of the Catholic Church*, no.135). For in the
Protestant camp the view of the Bible as the Word of God – in
contrast to the view just cited – is nowadays no longer usually
put forward in the literal sense. The preference is rather for
formulas like 'God's word in, with, under the human word' or
suchlike. Thus for example in the Protestant Adult Catechism
one can read: 'Christian faith lives on the fact that God speaks
and acts with human beings. The original and normative testimony is the Bible. Through the human word it expresses God's
Word' (1975: 39f.); 'God's word *does not stand behind the
words* of the Bible, so that we must first distil it from them; God
speaks to us *in the word* of the Bible as it is; here he allows
himself to be found by us' (1266). The present Bishop of
Hanover, Horst Hirschler, put it in a similarly way in an interview in the *Sonntagsblatt*, which he himself edits (8/1996: 29),
when he said that every theologian learns 'at the beginning of
his study that the Word of God is contained in the Bible as
human word'. But precisely what does God and Word of God
mean here? Does God actually *speak*? Certainly the prophets
say that God has commissioned them to address his Word to

particular people. But we must immediately add, 'the prophets *thought* that this was the case'. We know that they only thought in this way. In other words, this was their own interpretation of a religious experience. It is a long way from this to the claim that here God has really spoken, and one that is difficult for people after the Enlightenment to follow.

The harmonization of the biblical writings

A firm protest must be made against the harmonization of the biblical writings which in fact takes place in the preface to the revised Luther Bible, since in the Bible so much stands by side which was originally meant to be exclusive. Thus a forger wrote II Thessalonians from the start as a replacement for I Thessalonians and audaciously called the latter a forgery in order to guarantee the success of his undertaking (cf. Lüdemann 1996: 108–20). Furthermore, in respect of the four Gospels the well-founded suspicion arises that the Gospel of John was not meant to supplement but to *replace* the three earlier Gospels, Matthew, Mark and Luke (cf. Windisch 1926). Matthew and Luke again used the Gospel of Mark, not so that from then on there should be several Gospels side by side, but in order to offer their particular church the *one* valid Gospel writing. Some subsequent Christian generations rewarded them, since *after* the composition of the Gospels of Matthew and Luke and their dissemination the Gospel of Mark was used extraordinarily rarely. This only changed when the Gospel of Mark became one of the four Gospels and subsequently part of the canon. However, the moment the biblical documents were canonized, they ceased to exist as individual testimonies. Compare the view of Franz Overbeck:

> It is the nature of all canonization to make its objects unknowable, and so one can also say of all the writings of our New Testament that they ceased to be understood the moment they were canonized. They were transposed into the higher sphere of an eternal norm for the church, not without

a thick veil being laid over their origin, their original relationships and their original meaning (1880: 1).

So what are we to do? Read the individual documents and attempt to understand them? In that case the canon ought to be abolished. Read the documents in the framework of the canon (cf. the examples in Lüdemann 1996: 270 n.297)? In that case we are practising an exegesis which goes against the individual testimonies, which should be excluded out of respect for the people who were writing and speaking at that time. The aporia in the present treatment of the Bible in scholarship and also in the official church formally cries out for another approach to it.

In the interest of honesty, first all attempts should be abandoned to understand the Bible as both the human word and the Word of God. For which part of the Bible represents the human word and which the Word of God? Moreover, here it is not noted that God always appears only in speech and action communicated by human beings. In other words, we are always dealing only with *images* of God, with human claims that God has acted or spoken here or there. Anyone who says that the Bible contains the word of man *and* the Word of God is making use of the same unclear terminology which also occurs in thoughtless talk of the 'cross *and* resurrection of Jesus'. In both cases the human word and the Word of God, cross and resurrection, are, to use Ludwig Wittgenstein's terminology, parallel in surface grammar, but different in depth grammar. The human word and the cross denote historical facts, the Word of God and resurrection their interpretations. Accordingly the two expressions 'human word and Word of God' and 'cross and resurrection' suggest a parallel which does not exist at all. Unprejudiced hearers simply see themselves being deceived as soon as they are enlightened about the true situation.

Refutability as a criterion for a scientific statement

When theologians nowadays speak thoughtlessly of the action of God, they do not make it clear that outside theology, in history and philology, no one speaks any longer of God's action in history. And this is a good thing, since in any case God was too often introduced as a God of the gaps, who served to defend one's own view against others.

It cannot be said often enough that God is not an object of historical or scientific research, unless the entity designated God were falsifiable. Therefore the attempt to understand the Bible as human word and Word of God is apologetic through and through. It can never be refuted on the side which is related to God.

All scientific statements always have only a hypothetical character. Scholarly concerns are therefore decisively focussed on exposing their hypotheses and sketches to testing. It must always be possible to confront their consequences with the actual facts. Certainly interpretation is always involved in any observation, but any progress in knowledge comes closer to the actual facts.

At this point Hans Albert has made his theoretical scientific objections to philosophy and theology. He atttacks all attempts to seek to derive sure knowledge from ultimate certainties. He is particularly critical of the 'understanding reason' which offers itself to theology as a handmaid.

In this context a fundamental distinction is often claimed between faith and knowledge. In the sphere of knowledge, above all in science, reason, rational thought, seems to have quite a different function from that which it has in the sphere of so-called faith. Whereas a critical reason is in place in the first sphere, in the second the tendency seems more to be in favour of an interpretative, understanding, hermeneutical reason or even completely to dismiss the procedures of reason which are adequate here ... In this sphere, in some circumstances people are even prepared to put logic out of action so that genuine contradictions become acceptable (Albert 1973: 25).

Albert's basic criticism is also correct where theology is concerned: a sphere of ultimate certainties can be produced artificially with hermeneutical procedures, i.e. procedures concerned with understanding. Often an arbitrary frontier is also drawn between core thoughts to be preserved and incidental matters which can be exposed to discussion and criticism. This breaking off of discussion, thus given hermeneutical support, is crowned with a whole legion of variants. The crass difference between them perplexes readers: the arbitrariness with which a line is drawn between the core notion that is to be dogmatized and the peripheral material that is to be subjected to criticism is boundless. Texts can be totally protected from criticism since they only serve as *bases* for our understanding. This basic role all too quickly leads to their alleged unassailability. The consequence of this is that our present-day criticism, which is unavoidable where texts are concerned, cannot be applied to change them, but is always expressed in the guise of interpretation (cf. Albert 1973: 18). This 'masquerade' of interpretation makes honest criticism of the texts impossible and no longer takes them seriously as documents of their own time.

Regarded in this way, Rudolf Bultmann's enterprise of demythologizing also looks like a rearguard action. Its function consists in making what Bultmann regards as kerygma, i.e. as preaching, unassailable, namely immune from all criticism. Thus he wants to rescue the alleged core of Christian faith by an interpretation which harmonizes it with the present world-view. What is problematical, however, is that Bultmann interprets the saving event as an act of God. But this interpretation is already the *result* of his existentialist interpretation. His talk of God's action is simply empty when he interprets the cosmological picture of the world that corresponds to the kerygma, the only picture in which a historical action of God is plausible, in existentialist terms and replaces cosmology with anthropology.

Now in this context the notion of the resurrection which is

destined for rescue or dogmatization is so completely evacuated that it can no longer clash with any possible fact. It ends up as a shell, with no trace of empirical content.

As an example of a crude and forced way of raising the notion of the resurrection into the cloudy spheres of dogma one might draw attention to the conversation between Werner Harenberg of *Der Spiegel* and the former Göttingen New Testament professor Hans Conzelmann, on which Albert comments (1969: 126 n.59). To the question whether or not Jesus is risen, Conzelmann replies:

> 'Anyone who asks this sort of question ... is in reality not asking but already knows in advance what resurrection is' – what an ... astonishing statement! If one asks whether Spartacus led a revolt, one presumably also 'knows in advance what a revolt is', i.e. how the word 'revolt' is to be used. He then continues, 'The question whether the resurrection is a historical fact, whether it is an event in time and space, is completely meaningless. Only one thing is of essential importance, namely that the crucified one is not annihilated, that he is there... that he is the Lord, and that the world thus stands under the determination of the cross. For the risen one is the crucified one. We can see him only as such.'

On this Albert remarks:

> The arrogance with which the question is rejected is striking. In the end it could be dictated by a simple interest in making out what one should believe as a Christian today. Possible a to some degree specific, though naive, notion is also associated with 'resurrection', of the kind which presumably most Christians have had to the present day. And one is then dismissed by an expert with the thesis that the question is meaningless ... What is then brought out as of essential significance is certainly no clearer than the question of the resurrection. But really the only person who can claim that this is not significant is someone who is completely

indifferent as to whether the statements of the Bible have any truth-value in the usual sense. From the semantic perspective Conzelmann's answer is at least as naive as the question which he so arrogantly dismisses. Extremely painful questions are associated with each of his statements, which can be suppressed here only because the sloppiness which has crept in under the influence of hermeneutical irrationalism seems to keep them away (Albert 1969: 126f. n.59).

Finally, Gerhard Ebeling's and Wolfhart Pannenberg's discussions with Hans Albert do not seem to have brought the hoped-for clarity either.

Pannenberg fundamentally endorsed Albert's approach, but at the same time attempted to escape him again immediately through the back door. He would not have it that individual historical events were open to Albert's criticism (Pannenberg 1976: 67ff.). Instead, he claimed that their temporally determined unique individuality and their contingent sequence made them unrepeatable and thus not finally open to examination by verification or falsification. Here he was arguing on the unexpressed presupposition that the resurrection of Jesus which he postulates is also in fact a singular historical event which cannot be examined by human beings. But the general consensus is that the historical 'event' of the resurrection goes back to visions of the first disciples (cf. Lüdemann 1994), so that Pannenberg's presupposition is more than questionable, indeed absurd.

Ebeling allowed himself to be led astray into many pointed statements against Albert's critical rationalism which unfortunately hardly touched on the level at which Albert was concerned for clarification. His response to Albert (Ebeling 1973) once again demonstrates vividly how justified Albert's sharp criticism of Protestant theology is. In it Ebeling declares quite forthrightly: 'To argue with the possession or even the unattainability of a standpoint which is absolute and therefore at the same time universal misses our actual situation of knowing and living in an infinite context of the finite' (Ebeling 1973: 3).

What does Ebeling mean here? Does he not see that there is a great difference between whether one thinks one can adopt a universal and certain standpoint or whether one joins Albert in arguing that this is unattainable? Ebeling's awareness of the finitude of all knowledge in the infinite context of life cannot long hold up the distinction between possessing an assured standpoint and criticism of this position. Or does Ebeling even think that we should wholly dispense with any meaningful argumentation in favour of this insight?

The conclusion to be drawn is that Albert's epistemological objections to the hermeneutical undertakings in theology are still far from being answered. The countless points at which discussion is broken off in theology are still disguised with semantic craftiness, in order to withdraw from the sphere of critical philosophical examination favourite convictions which are thought to be particularly important, like those of the resurrection of Jesus or the character of the Bible as the human word and the Word of God. Safeguarding the truths of faith once they have been attained has priority over any critical examination. All too often in contemporary theological literature the necessary intellectual clarity is sacrificed in favour of an attempt to coax assent to the dogmas of the human word and the Word of God in the Bible and the resurrection of Jesus. However, in the end this only cements a person's own uncertainty against any possible progress in knowledge. Alternative profane explanatory hypotheses cannot find any space in the context of a dogmatically motivated break in the discussion, let alone clear criticisms of religion like those of Ludwig Feuerbach or Friedrich Nietzsche, and therefore cannot contribute anything to the new beginning for theology and church which will be ultimately necessary.

The pre-critical use of the Bible in the memorandum Believing Today *of the German Protestant Church*

To the present day, official Protestantism as a church of the Reformation ties its understanding of being a Christian closely to the Bible. Thus *Believing Today. Becoming a Christian –*

Remaining a Christian, a writing which was published in a large edition in 1988 on behalf of the Synod of the Evangelical Church in Germany, deals right at the beginning with what a Christian is in the biblical sense, since we 'learn from the Bible what being a Christian consists of' (13), and 'Christians are first of all people who are concerned to be Christians in the biblical sense' (12). However, there then follows a collection of biblical quotations which indicate merely a highly selective use of the Bible; not a single insight of historical biblical criticism appears in this memorandum published for the Christian churches and the general public, although biblical scholars were also involved in producing it.

The counter-test for this quite astonishing statement is the question whether the parts of this writing relating to the Bible could also have been composed in the sixteenth century. The answer to this is certainly yes.

The memorandum states: 'Christians expect the kingdom of God and focus their lives on it' (11). This conceals the fact that the expectation of the kingdom of God among the first Christians, who at the same time understood themselves as *the last* Christians, was disappointed. The clearest indication of the imminent expectation of the end by Christians is Paul's first letter to the Thessalonians. In ch.4 Paul takes it for granted that the then members of the community will survive until Jesus' return. Verse 15 states, 'we who are alive until the coming of the Lord'; v.17, 'we who are alive, who are left' (cf. Lüdemann 1996: 78–84). But in that case why should Christians living two thousand years later still wait for the kingdom of God? That is the burning question for present-day men and women. They will not be led by the nose with the statement in the memorandum quoted above but expect honest answers before instructions about who is a Christian today.

The memorandum states: 'Christians are first of all people who are concerned to be Christians in the biblical sense' (12). This statement is unclear as long as the term 'biblical sense' is not explained. The following questions arise. Does that mean the whole Bible? Only the New Testament? As emerges from the context in the memorandum, 'biblical sense' is focussed on the discipleship of Jesus (12f.). But what is that meant to look like in the present? And how is discipleship of Jesus related to discipleship of the risen Christ? Of that the authors of the memorandum write: Jesus Christ 'is our living Lord, who calls us to be his disciples' (18). The living Lord calls us to be disciples? The living Lord or the risen Christ who sits at the right hand of God – how can I still be a disciple of this heavenly being today? Here the memorandum associates things which are not compatible.

A further statement runs: 'We believe that Jesus Christ has died on the cross for us ... In the complaint "My God, my God, why have you forsaken me?" he nevertheless held fast to God. God has raised Jesus Christ from the dead' (18). Here three historically questionable fragments stand side by side undigested:

(a) The death for us is incomprehensible at least as an atoning death, and is moreover historically dubious, since Jesus certainly did not want to die for the sins of the world. The statements about the atoning power of Jesus' death are interpretations by the community and were put on to the lips of Jesus subsequently (for a summary cf. Friedrich 1982).

(b) Jesus did not utter the cry on the cross. On the one hand it contradicts other exclamations of his on the cross, cf. Luke 23.46, 'Father, into your hands I commend my spirit' (Ps. 31.6); John 19.30, 'It is finished.' On the other hand Jesus' cry in 14.34 is 'a secondary interpretation of 15.37 ... where it is simply the occurrence of a loud cry that is recorded' (Bultmann 1968: 313). This secondary interpretation was orientated on Ps. 22.2, just as the crucifixion was secondarily enriched by borrowings from the Old Testament Psalter, cf. Mark 15.24/ Ps. 22.19; Mark 15.27/Isa. 53.12; Mark 15.29/Ps. 22.8; Mark 15.36/Ps. 69.22. 'If we read the Psalms which have supplied most material for the Passion narrative, i.e. Psalms 22, 31, 69, we are struck in all three by the mention of the cry (22.25; 31.23; 69.4)' (Dibelius 1934: 187). These passages shaped the narrative about the hour of Jesus' death. The fact that in Mark

Jesus' cry is given in its Aramaic version does not tell in favour of its historicity but rather against it: it is impossible that the Roman soldiers could have heard the cry 'Elohi', etc. handed down from the Aramaic as a prayer to Elijah (thus Mark 15.35). Matthew (27.46) has removed this difficulty and turned 'Elohi' into 'Eli'.

(c) The 'resurrection of Jesus' is unclear as long as we are not told precisely what is meant by this. Is it a historical event which presupposes the revival of the corpse? Or did the disciples only have visions? Did these come from God in a different way from other visions, or are they to be regarded as ways of assimilating the death of Jesus (for these questions see Lüdemann 1994 and the informative account by Zager 1996). Anyone who speaks of the 'resurrection of Jesus' as naively as the authors of the memorandum is open to the suspicion of treating the resurrection only as an indispensable requisite of theology and thus as an empty formula.

The conclusion to be drawn is that in its biblical basis the memorandum is pre-critical or pre-modern and not suitable for promoting real study of the Bible, far less arousing interest in Holy Scripture. So it is high time to understand the Bible in a human way, to arouse it like a Sleeping Beauty and thoroughly to do away with the monopolistic claim which the Christian churches and large areas of so-called academic theology have successfully established in their highly selective biblical exegesis.

The divisions in this book

Unlike the majority of the interpreters of the Bible I shall approach it from its dark, unknown, ugly, suppressed side. I shall take the author of the preface to the revised Luther translation at his word, that the Bible seeks to offer the good news of God's mercy to all human beings, and examine it to see whether historically that was really the case and still is the case today.

The second chapter, which follows, deals with the Old Testament. It is prefaced by a sketch of the history of Israel and a chronological framework of the events presupposed in the Old

Testament and of the writings contained in it, which is based on the consensus of scholars. Then follows an analysis of texts which reflect a quite different picture of the Old Testament from the view that in it the good news of God's mercy is communicated to all men and women. It covers those parts which contain God's command to exterminate whole peoples.

In a third chapter I turn to the New Testament, and as in the Old Testament part first offer a sketch of the history of early Christianity, with an introduction to the problems of the earliest church and a chronological survey which takes into account the state of international scholarship at present. Then, as in the second chapter, follow individual investigations of texts which similarly indicate little of God's mercy. They relate to those passages which describe the unbelieving Jews of the time as enemies of God and exclude them from God's mercy on the spot.

These observations on structure may at first sound rather abstract. Only an extended discussion, quotation and historical rooting of the relevant texts will bring particular situations alive and provide a stimulus for learning, rethinking and indeed enlightenment. This preliminary work is necessary, since for centuries the Bible has been read only in an ecclesiastical and dogmatic framework, and even today people only rarely encounter what it actually contains.

Under the title 'Jesus and the Mercy of God', a fourth chapter discusses the question how in view of this ruinous other side of Holy Scripture it can be possible for us to go on being Christians today and commends resolute reflection on Jesus of Nazareth.

A fifth chapter criticizes the church of today on the basis of what has been worked out and makes suggestions about how to deal with the present crisis.

The one-sidednesses of this book and the reasons for them. Enlightenment as an aim worth striving for in theology

In this book I have deliberately been one-sided. This is necessary because of a widespread partisan attitude to the Bible and the deceit which is associated with that. It is also necessary in the interest of truth. For that, too, is part of the tragedy of our present-day situation. Those predominantly preoccupied with the Bible earn their living from it; in addition there are five to ten per cent of the members of the Christian churches who take an active part in community life. The other ninety per cent, who in countries like German finance the institution by their church tax, have long ceased to believe what the minority tell them about the Bible, and consume only the isolated sayings which are presented to them at the great festivals and festivities. But partisanship or eclecticism are not an appropriate basis for a real encounter with the Bible. Precisely for that reason, for the sake of the Bible we need an *independent* criticism of Holy Scripture and the churches which claim it for themselves.

This criticism has to consider both the content of the Bible and also the claims to authority which the church associates with it. It is obligated to the Enlightenment and calls on all to make use of their *own* understanding (Kant 1966: 53). Immanuel Kant combines with his slogan of enlightenment a demand which similarly has far-reaching consequences.

It is important 'to make public use of one's reason in all things' (Kant 1966: 55). The use of one's own reason for critical examination has a public character. However, according to Kant one can make use of this right to *public reason* as a scholar only in contrast to the *private reason* of the social functionary – a distinction which can no longer be maintained in a democratic society. Anyone who relieves officials and functionaries in business, the army, state and church who feel obligated to private reason of their responsibility towards universal public reason, which today feels a commitment to the survival of humankind, should be reminded of the reaction

by Günther Anders in the face of the world-wide atomic
threat:

> In a democracy we have the guaranteed right as cobblers,
> doctors, miners, management, workers or students to have a
> say in decisions which have nothing to do with our depart-
> ment of work: 'Anyone who limits the conscience of citizens
> to the departments assigned to them, to their offices or their
> fields of work, is replacing the conscience with a mere
> conscientiousness which could remain even in extermination
> camps and did indeed remain there. As we have no reason to
> presuppose that the demarcation lines drawn "conscien-
> tiously" owe their existence and their course to moral
> principles, the decisive function of our conscience lies pre-
> cisely in ignoring the limits of competence. That is true of
> everyone ... and not just of us scholars ... The call of our
> conscience no more knows an "as" than the conscience of our
> non-academic fellow men and women' (Anders 1972: 27).

In all conscience, this public responsibility cannot be limited
by pressures and claims to authority in departments and preserves. Accordingly, it must not be restricted in the church
sphere either. Nor is this fact altered if officials there can appeal
to the specific division of work in society or beyond that to the
authority of the Bible.

Falk Wagner has rightly pointed out the need to examine all
claims to authority critically before the forum of the reason of
the modern consciousness. 'The authority of tradition, the
magisterium and the biblical writings which was presupposed
without question by mediaeval scholastic thought can be
formulated under the condition of reason and autonomous
thought only as a *claim* to authority which first of all has to be
grounded, justified and controlled' (1995: 69f.), if we are not
once again to bid farewell to thinking for ourselves and taking
responsibility for ourselves.

Consequences for the theological faculties of the future

If enlightenment is a goal worth striving for in theology also, it is clear that real progress can be expected only if there is parity in the occupation of posts carrying a responsibility for biblical exegesis. To be specific, only if future theological faculties have an equal number of posts for scholars orientated on the church, and scholars from other religions and critics of religion (including atheists) can progress in knowledge be expected.

The present situation of so-called academic theology is quite obviously precarious because theology in Germany is organized confessionally, and even representatives of Protestant theology are concerned to go on supporting the confessional status of their faculties. This has happened recently, for example, when lecturers and newly-appointed professors in Göttingen have once again to take the following oath from the year 1846: 'I pledge myself to present the theological disciplines honestly, clearly and thoroughly, in accord with the principles of the Evangelical Lutheran Church.' This contradicts the expectation expressed, when lecturers are given authority to teach in the university, that they will be concerned 'to do their best as academic teachers and researchers to serve scholarship and to educate the academic youth in the spirit of truth'. Catholic counterparts will delight in this reorientation, since for them the magisterium of the church applies anyway. But let's not be deceived. If, as happens in Göttingen, the Protestant faculties in Germany tie themselves closely to the church's confession, they have in fact been turned into Roman Catholic faculties. The details of the dogmatic differences will no longer matter, since a tie to a confession excludes really free scholarship, however much one may claim to be working in a true academic fashion.

Legally, at any rate, the present position is clear. The freedom of a Protestant theologian to engage in research and to teach ends where he or she comes into conflict with the doctrine of the church. Thus the author of a standard book about the theological faculties in a secular democratic state, Martin Heckel, writes: 'A teacher of theology certainly has the liberal freedom to deviate (sic!) from the theological obligations of his office, which he promised voluntarily and with full knowledge to fulfil – but in no way does he have the "freedom" (i.e. permission to intervene) to pervert the doctrine of his church against its will by his state teaching office' (1986: 169).

Certainly in defence of the Göttingen oath one could point out that 'confession' is not to be identified with 'principle' and therefore that the Göttingen obligation quoted above does not necessarily state a tie to the confession of the Evangelical Lutheran Church. But what can 'principle' mean, if not 'confession'? The principle of freedom of conscience? But in that case such an oath is not needed, since freedom of conscience is guaranteed by the Basic Law of the Federal Republic of Germany (art. 4).

I would like to state the principle like this: as long as there is a Protestant *and* a Catholic theology at the universities in Germany, it is evident that theology is not a true academic discipline. With Paul de Lagarde, we can also put it like this.

Anyone who knows scholarship knows that it is an end in itself and therefore seeks its own methods, and does not accept precepts, laws and aims from any power in heaven or on earth. It seeks to know, nothing but to know and only to know. It knows that it does not know anything which it has not proved. What emerges from his investigations is a matter of complete indifference to any scholar, i.e. as long as new truths are discovered. Scholarship allows anyone to re-examine the results it discovers and ruthlessly rejects anything that does not stand up to such an examination. It requires of anyone who has the necessary prior qualifications to judge that he accept and acknowledge what has been proved to him or give up any claim to being an honest man.

One can easily be convinced that this description of scholarship cannot be applied to the discipline which we in Germany call theology and that therefore theology as practised at present is not a true academic discipline (Lagarde 1920: 40f.).

From this it follows automatically that well-founded criticism of church and theology in Germany can predominantly be practised only on the basis of another regular activity. This is an enormous disadvantage in the face of the large number of people whose main professional involvement or interest is bound up with the church or theology and who therefore willingly or unwillingly maintain the present situation (cf. Buggle 1992: 16). There is something cowardly here, even from the external point of view.

But the inner substance of the criticism of dogmas and the church practices by professional theologians is disturbingly weak The public in Germany regard the dissidents Hans Küng, Uta Ranke-Heinemann and Eugen Drewermann as enlightened people. However, as Christoph Türcke emphasizes, they have little in common with this name. Türcke comments: 'One has only to ask whether there is such a God as they decree, whether the certainties that they cherish about his oneness or multiplicity, his gender, his involvement in what happens in the world or his final victory at the last day is not simple arrogance ... and their whole modernity already fades. They too brace themselves on their iron ration of faith ... and behave no less fundamentalistically than their opponents in the ranks of the church' (1992, 16). Radical thought 'which goes to the root of things has collapsed' (Türcke 1992: 68). This is one more reason, in the interest of historical truth *and* of what is really Christian, to make a new attempt to regard the Holy Scripture of the Christian churches in a different way from usual.

2

Unholy Violence against Others in the New Testament and the Reason for It

A. An outline of the history of Israel

Introduction

The history of Israel as contained in the Old Testament covers a span of more than 1000 years, from the nomadic period (cf. Gen. 12–50) around 1500–1300 BCE to the turmoil surrounding the desecration of the Jerusalem temple by the Syrian king Antiochus IV in the middle of the second century BCE, to which the book of Daniel is a reaction.

Given such an enormous period of time it is a priori likely that a variety of groups shaped 'the' religion of Israel – particularly also in view of the far-reaching revolutions which Israel experienced in this period. The greatest trauma was the loss of an independent state and the ensuing exile in Babylon (587–539 BCE). So it is no coincidence that there is no historiography of this in the Old Testament, whereas there are narratives about all the other periods, though their historical value still needs to be clarified in detail.

Here I shall give a chronological survey of the history of Israel orientated on the consensus of scholars (cf. Kaiser 1992: 22f.). I have not taken account here of the redating (i.e. late dating) of Old Testament writings, which leads to a complete devaluation of the Old Testament as a historical source (for this see the somewhat helpless report by Herrmann 1991).

The following books are important for the discussion which

has newly opened up and for the history of Israel: Lemche 1985; Davies 1995; there is conservative anti-criticism in Provan 1995.

A word on terminology. In contrast to most translations of the Bible, which transcribe the Hebrew name God as 'LORD', here I shall regularly use the probably original form Yahweh. However, as written ancient Hebrew has no real vowels, only the consonants YHWH, the so-called tetragrammaton, are certain.

The reason why the pronunciation of this name can no longer be established with one hundred per cent certainty but only with some probability from the short form *Yah* (e.g. in *Hallelu-yah* – 'praise Yahweh') and from old Greek texts is that at a very early stage, in the pre-Christian period, Judaism forbade its use for fear that the second commandment (Ex. 20.7; Deut. 5.11) could be violated. At the time of Jesus the name was pronounced only in temple worship, at the priestly blessing and on the Day of Atonement in the penitential prayers of the high priest in the innermost forecourt of the temple, so that no Gentile could hear it. In synagogue worship the name YHWH was replaced by *'adonay'* (Lord), and the Septuagint, the Greek translation of the Old Testament, reproduces YHWH with *kyrios* (= Lord). The avoidance of the divine name was carried through so consistently that probably soon after the destruction of the Jerusalem temple (70 CE), all recollection of the correct pro-nunciation of the Tetragrammaton disappeared and from then on the divine name only existed as a sign and no longer as a spoken word (cf. Kuhn 1938: 93).

The Jewish scholars who later provided the Hebrew text with vowel signs kept the component YHWH, but added, as a reminder of the substitute used, the vowels of the Hebrew word for Lord (*adonay*, with the initial *a* abbreviated to *e*) instead of the original vowels. As a result of a misunderstanding this later became the artificial word Jehovah, first used by Calvin and the Calvinists.

Chronological framework

NOMADIC PREHISTORY: FIFTEENTH (?) – THIRTEENTH CENTURIES

PERIOD BEFORE THE STATE: TWELFTH – ELEVENTH CENTURIES
  Settlement, cultivation of the land, Israel as a tribal alliance

MONARCHY: C. 1000–587

Time of the undivided kingdom: c. 1000–926
  Saul, David (capital Jerusalem), Solomon (building of the temple)

Time of the divided kingdoms: 926–722
  926: so-called division of the kingdom (Northern Kingdom Israel, Southern Kingdom Judah)
  (first firm date in the history of Israel: I Kings 12)
  pressure on Israel from the Aramaean kingdom (esp. 850–800), Elijah, Elisha
  Assyrian domination (c.750–610) – Amos (c.760)
  c. 733: Syro-Ephraimite war against Judah (II Kings 16.5; Isa. 7); Hosea (c.750–725), Isaiah (c.740–700)

Kingdom of Judah: 722–587
  722: Conquest of Samaria by the Assyrians (II Kings 17)
  701: Siege of Jerusalem by the Assyrians (II Kings 18–20 = Isa. 36–39)
  c.622: Josiah's reform (II Kings 22f.; Deut.), Jeremiah (c.626–586)
  612: Conquest of the Assyrian capital Nineveh by the Babylonians
  609: Death of Josiah in battle against the Egyptian king Pharaoh Necho (II Kings 23.29f.), who had freed himself from Assyrian domination
  597: First destruction of Jerusalem by the Babylonians – Ezekiel

BABYLONIAN EXILE: 587–539

587: Final destruction of Jerusalem by the Babylonians (II Kings 24f.; Jer. 27ff.), Lamentations, Deuteronomic History: Deut.-II Kings (c.560), Priestly Writing, Deutero-Isaiah

POST-EXILIC PERIOD: 539–64

Persian domination: 539–333
539: Fall of Babylon to the Persians (Isa. 46f. etc.)
530: Trito-Isaiah
520–535: Rebuilding of the temple (Ezra 5f.), Haggai, Zechariah
458 (or 398): Ezra
445–433: Nehemiah

Hellenistic period: 333 BCE –70 CE
333: Victory of Alexander the Great over the Persians, Chronistic History
164: Reconsecration of the temple during the Maccabaean revolt, Daniel
64: Conquest of Palestine by the Romans
70 CE: Destruction of Jerusalem

B. The ban in the Holy War – a gesture of mercy?

By way of qualification I should begin by pointing out that the texts mentioned below come from different times. Thus Deut. 1–3 as an introduction to the Deuteronomistic history (cf. Perlitt 1994, 109–22: 119–22 on the 'conceptional unity' of this chapter) is at least a century later than the passage from Deut. 4.44ff. (for Deut. 4.1–4, 43 cf. Noth 1963: *ad loc.*). First we are concerned only with the phenomenon of the ban; the historical question of its time and context will be raised in the course of the analyses.

The phenomenon of the Holy War

There is hardly anything in the Old Testament which provokes the abhorrence of the modern observer so much as the practice of the ban as the conclusion of a 'Holy War'. Here some texts gathered from different periods give an indication of what this ban involved.

Numbers 21.1–3: 1 When the Canaanites who dwelt in the Negeb heard that Israel was coming by the way of Atharim, they fought against Israel, and took some of them captive. 2 And Israel vowed a vow to Yahweh and said, 'If you will indeed give this people into my hand, then I will utterly destroy their cities.' 3 And Yahweh hearkened to the voice of Israel, and gave over the Canaanites; and they utterly destroyed them and their cities; so the name of the place was called Hormah (= ban).

Deuteronomy 2.30–35: 30 But Sihon the king of Heshbon would not let us pass by him; for Yahweh your God hardened his spirit and made his heart obstinate, that he might give him into your hand, as at this day. 31 And Yahweh said to me, 'Behold, I have begun to give Sihon and his land over to you; begin to take possession, that you may occupy his land.' 32 Then Sihon came out against us, he and all his people, to battle at Jahaz. 33 And Yahweh our God gave him over to us; and we defeated him and his sons and all his people. 34 And we captured all his cities at that time and utterly destroyed every city, men, women, and children; we left none remaining; 35 only the cattle we took as spoil for ourselves, with the booty of the cities which we captured.

Deuteronomy 3.3–7: 3 So Yahweh our God gave into our hand Og also, the king of Bashan, and all his people; and we smote him until no survivor was left to him. 4 And we took all his cities at that time – there was not a city which we did not take from them – sixty cities, the whole region of Argob, the kingdom of Og in Bashan. 5 All these were cities fortified with high walls, gates, and bars, besides very many unwalled villages. 6 And we utterly destroyed them, as we did to Sihon the king of Heshbon, destroying every city, men, women, and children. 7 But all the cattle and the spoil of the cities we took as our booty.

Deuteronomy 7.1–2: 1 When Yahweh your God brings you into the land which you are entering to take possession of it, and clears away many nations before you, the Hittites, the Girgashites, the Amorites, the Canaanites, the Perizzites, the Hivites, and the Jebusites, seven nations greater and mightier than yourselves, 2 and when Yahweh your God gives them over to you, and you defeat them; then you must utterly destroy them; you shall make no covenant with them, and show no mercy to them.

Joshua 6.17–21: 17 'But this city (= Jericho) and all that is within it shall be devoted to Yahweh for destruction; only Rahab the harlot and all who are with her in her house shall live, because she hid the messengers that we sent. 18 But you, keep yourselves from the things devoted to destruction, lest when you have devoted them you take any of the devoted things and make the camp of Israel a thing for destruction, and bring trouble upon it. 19 But all silver and gold, and vessels of bronze and iron, are sacred to Yahweh; they shall go into the treasury of Yahweh.' 20 So the people shouted, and the trumpets were blown. As soon as the people heard the sound of the trumpet, the people raised a great shout, and the wall fell down flat, so that the people went up into the city, every man straight before him, and they took the city. 21 Then they utterly destroyed all in the city, both men and women, young and old, oxen, sheep, and asses with the edge of the sword.

Joshua 10.28: And Joshua took Makkedah on that day, and smote it and its king with the edge of the sword; he utterly destroyed every person in it, he left none remaining; and he did to the king of Makkedah as he had done to the king of Jericho.

Joshua 11.10–11: 10 And Joshua took Hazor, and smote its king with the sword; for Hazor formerly was the head of all those kingdoms. 11 And they put to the sword all who were in it, utterly destroying them; and there was none left that breathed, and he burned Hazor with fire.

According to Gerhard von Rad's theory, the ban in ancient Israel was part of the institution of the Holy War (for what follows see von Rad 1991:41–51). This was governed by the following acts: the army was raised by the blowing of the trumpet (Judg. 6.34f.; cf. Judg. 3.27; I Sam. 13.3), or by a particularly archaic feature, the sending out of chunks of flesh (I Sam. 11.7), and gathered in the camp where the warriors, from then on called 'the people of Yahweh' (Judg. 5.11,13; 20.2), prepared for the impending battle with cultic purification, sexual asceticism, sacrifices and penitential rites.

Before the beginning of the battle enquiry is made of Yahweh, who forecasts victory in an oracle. Thereupon the leader makes a proclamation to the army ('Yahweh has given the ... into your hand'; cf. Josh. 2.24; Judg. 3.28, etc.) and the army marches against the enemy with Yahweh at its head. The battle opens with war cries and shouting. This Yahweh terror which befalls the enemy and confuses them, so that their courage fails, brings victory. 'The high point and conclusion was the *ban:* the consecration of the booty to Yahweh. As is the case for the entire holy war, this too is a cultic phenomenon: human beings and animals are slaughtered; gold, silver, and the like go ... into Yahweh's treasury (Josh. 6.18f.)' (von Rad 1991: 49).

Anyone who reads the texts about the ban and the slaughter of foreign peoples today without prejudice can only be disturbed about them. Around a century ago Ernest Renan expressed his abhorrence of these 'barbarous customs dripping with blood' as follows: 'Human cruelty took the form of a pact with the deity. A solemn oath was made to kill everything, in which people forbade themselves any display of reason or compassion. A city or a land was devoted to destruction and it was believed an insult to God if one did not observe the abominable oath' (Renan 1894: 232).

The ban is not revenge, but a ritual

Nevertheless, following Barr (1993: 208–21), it has to be pointed out that the devotion to destruction did not arise out of personal hatred or vengeance. Rather, it was a kind of sacrificial ritual in which the population of the conquered cities were often exterminated, even with their animals. Furthermore indestructible objects of gold or silver could not be kept as plunder by just anyone. Rather, they were regarded as gifts for the God of Israel. Moreover, the Hebrew word for 'ban' (*ḥrm*) belongs in the semantic field of the holy, hallowed, which in fact justifies the translation 'consecration to destruction'. It is then the negative side of the holy, the content of which is making something inaccessible to general use, whereas the better known Hebrew expression for the holy, *qds*, indicates its positive qualities, those to be preserved. Thus a person could consecrate an animal or a field to Yahweh and these might then no longer be put to normal use.

In other words, *the ritual of the ban was virtually the negation of an ethic or simple plundering and exploitation.* It was a ritual sanctification in which the captured persons, animals and objects were dedicated to Yahweh, and the objects which were indestructible were simply handed over to the sanctuary. By having the persons handed over to him in the same way as the animal sacrifices, God received them back as giver of life. Doubtless it would have been preferable to keep the victims as slaves, since human beings were valuable, like oxen, sheep and other animals. For this reason the ban was sometimes broken. But that immediately brought down punishment on those concerned. The ban was a tabu which no one might transgress – not even a king like Saul. When he nevertheless did so, he was immediately stripped of his kingly dignity and rejected.

I Sam. 15.1–3, 7–9, 23: 1 And Samuel said to Saul, 'Yahweh sent me to anoint you king over his people Israel; now therefore hearken to the words of Yahweh. 2. Thus says Yahweh Sabaoth, "I will punish what Amalek did to Israel in opposing them on the way, when they came up out of Egypt. 3 Now go and smite Amalek, and utterly destroy all that they have; do not spare them, but kill both man and woman, infant and suckling, ox and sheep, camel and ass"' ... 7 And Saul defeated the Amalekites, from Havilah as far as Shur, which is east of Egypt. 8 And he took Agag the king of the Amalekites alive, and utterly destroyed all the people with the edge of the sword. 9 But Saul and the people spared Agag, and the best of the sheep and of the oxen and of the fatlings, and the lambs, and all that was good, and would not utterly destroy them; all that was despised and worthless they utterly destroyed ... 23 (Samuel to Saul:) 'Disobedience is as the sin of witchcraft, and stubbornness is as iniquity and idolatry. Because you have rejected the word of Yahweh, he has also rejected you from being king.'

The Holy War did not take place very frequently and has parallels in the ancient Near East

By way of qualifying the offensiveness of the ban it is sometimes said that the Holy War as described in Deuteronomy and Joshua probably never took place in that form. In many cases compromises were made with the inhabitants of the land, as is shown by the story of the deceit of the Gibeonites (Josh. 9): the Gibeonites deceived Joshua because they were afraid that their city would be destroyed, and made a covenant with Israel as though they came from distant lands. We are told to pass the same judgment when the first chapter of the book of Judges describes the defeated Canaanites as remaining in the land and providing forced labour.

Certainly there is considerable doubt about von Rad's general assumption that the theory and practice of the Holy War were rooted in a sacral tribal alliance from the time before the

Israelite monarchy (twelfth-eleventh century BCE), since the assumption of a political and military unity of Israel before and during the settlement called for by such an assumption does not stand up to criticism. The Göttingen Old Testament scholar Rudolf Smend sums up the scholarly consensus as follows: 'All Israel was not yet involved in the events in the wilderness from the exodus out of Egypt, and Palestine was not conquered all at once by an army under the command of Joshua, as the book of Joshua describes it, but in a series of actions by individual groups and tribes. Initially there was no great use of military force even on fairly regular occasions' (Smend 1987:125f.).

Moreover, according to the Heidelberg Old Testament scholar Manfred Weippert, adding to von Rad, it emerges 'that examples can also be adduced from Assyrian texts of most elements of the "theory of the holy war", and the gaps remaining here can largely be filled in from evidence from ancient Babylonia and the Hittites. There is comparative material for the levy of the troops by a bloody symbolic action, for oaths, sacrifices and discovery of the divine will before the campaign and battle, for the answer given to an enquiry by the deity in the form of an oracle of encouragement or salvation with a formula about giving the enemy into their hands, and a promise of support, and for the ideas which are connected with divine intervention against the enemy. There is full evidence for the latter among the Assyrians: the gods go ahead of the army, the Assyrian troops are those of the imperial god Assur, the war is the war of the gods, the enemies are their enemies, the enemies lose their courage and are in fear of God even before the real battle; and in the battle above all the gods fight, while the human beings come to their help' (Weippert 1972: 483f.).

The one element which it seems impossible to demonstrate anywhere in the ancient Near East, with one exception (cf. 44ff. below), is the phenomenon of the ban. The evidence from the Hittite and Amarna texts which come closest to it speak only of a destruction, and not of a ban (cf. Gevirtz 1963; Kang 1989). Certainly kindred terms with the same root ḥrm appear in the environment of Israel, but with the same exception (cf. below

44ff.), never 'with the same horrific content' (Dietrich and Link 1995: 196).

Accordingly, the institution of the Holy War is not just to be found only in Israel, but is indebted to ideas general in the ancient Near East. At the same time it has a theoretical element, the realization of which must be decided in individual instances. This is not to deny that there were frequent warlike clashes. The oldest evidence for this is the Song of Miriam (twelfth century): 'Sing to Yahweh, for he has triumphed gloriously; the horse and its rider he has thrown into the sea' (Ex. 15.20). Cf. also the almost equally old victory song of Deborah in Judg. 5, which ends with the words: 'So perish all your enemies, Yahweh! But may your friends be like the sun as he rises in his might' (v.31). It is also clear that the spiritual climate in which (king) David became great two hundred years later was stamped by battle and war. For the sake of simplicity I simply quote the classic description by Julius Wellhausen: 'Then and for centuries afterwards the prime expression of the life of the nation was war. It is war that makes peoples; war was the function in which the cohesion of the Israelite tribes was first confirmed, and as a national war it was also a holy business. Yahweh was the battle-cry of this warlike confederacy, the shortest expression of what united them and separated them from others. Israel means "El [God] fights", and Yahweh was the fighting El, from whom the nation took its name. Israel also stood to Yahweh in the same relationship as the neighbouring peoples to their gods. Yahweh always preserved something of this warlike neighbour. Even in a late period Yahweh is described as a kind of war god who arms himself with sword and shield, who utters the battle-cry like a hero, shoots his arrows, draws his sword, soaks his garments in blood, feasts on the fat of the slain, sucks up their marrow. The war camp, the cradle of the nation, was also the oldest sanctuary. Such was Israel and such was Yahweh' (Wellhausen 1958: 23f.).

Does the fact that the Holy War is only partially historical remove its abhorrent character?

But even if the tradition of the Holy War were in part a fiction, that would not sufficiently illuminate the phenomenon in itself. For the real problem is not whether the narratives are fact or fiction. It causes scandal that ritual destruction is commanded at all. It is offensive where 'man's concern for power or even only for self-assertion takes on a religious colouring in the form of the holy war' (Gunneweg 1978: 118). The texts quoted call for the total slaughter of the Canaanite population, and the execution of this command, e.g. at the conquest of Jericho, is specifically emphasized, as Josh. 6.21 shows: 'Then they utterly destroyed all in the city, both men and women, young and old, oxen, sheep, and asses, with the edge of the sword.'

If the account of the destruction of Jericho was pure fiction (cf. Fritz 1994, 65–69), it was one which found general assent. And although the Old Testament contains an abundance of depictions of war, there is not a single passage which explicitly criticizes the ban or disputes that it was ordained by Yahweh (cf. Barr 1993: 219). On the contrary, where the ban is mentioned, this always happens in close connection with Yahweh himself. So the ban is by no means incidental; it has a terrifyingly fundamental character. Cf. Josh. 11.20: 'For it was Yahweh's doing to harden their hearts that they should come against Israel in battle, in order that they should be utterly destroyed, and should receive no mercy but be exterminated, as the Lord commanded Moses' (cf. Perlitt 1972: 45).

A Moabite parallel to the ban attests its actual use in Israel

A Moabite inscription attests that the ban was not practised only in Israel. It was doubtless something shared with at least one neighbour and in fact on particular occasions was implemented against Israel. As this inscription is only known to scholars, I shall quote here the first eighteen of its thirty-four lines:

The translation follows that of E. Ullendorff, in D. Winton Thomas, *Documents from Old Testament Times*, 1958, with some modifications. The meaning of the words in capitals in the text cannot be precisely determined: DWD (line 12) is probably a deity or something comparable; MHRT (line 14) is (like Sharon), the name of either a place or a landscape.

(1) I (am) Mesha, son of KMSH[YT], king of Moab, the (2) Dibonite. My father was king over Moab thirty years and I became king (3) after my father. And I made this high place [sanctuary] for Chemosh in Qericho as (4) a sanctuary of salvation; for he saved me from all the kings and let me see my desire upon my adversaries.

Omri, (5) king of Israel, he oppressed Moab many days, for Chemosh was angry with his land. (6) And his son succeeded him and he too said, 'I will oppress Moab.' In my days he spoke [thus], (7) and I saw my desire upon him and upon his house, when Israel perished utterly for ever. And Omri had taken possession of the (8) land of Medeba and [Israel] dwelt in it his days and half the days of his son forty years; but (9) Chemosh dwelt in it in my days. And I [re]built Baal-meon and made in it the reservoir, and I [re]built (10) Kiryathon.

And the men of Gad had long dwelt in the land of Ataroth, and the king of (11) Israel had built Ataroth (10) for himself. (11) But I fought against the town and took it and I slew all the people (12) of the town, a spectacle for Chemosh and Moab. And I brought back from there the altar-hearth of DWD and I (13) dragged it before Chemosh at Qereyoth. And I settled there the men of Sharon and the men (14) of MHRT.

And Chemosh said to me, 'Go, take Nebo (in battle) against Israel.' And (15) I went by night and fought against it from the break of dawn till noon; and I took it and slew all: seven thousand men, boys, women, and [girls] and (17) female slaves, for I had consecrated it to Ashtar-Chemosh (by the ban, *ḥrm*). And I took from there the [vessel]s(?) of (18) Yahweh and dragged them before Chemosh ...'

This inscription, which was found near Diban (in Transjordan) in 1868, comes from around the year 830 BCE. Mesha and his revolt against Israel are also mentioned in II Kings 3 (vv.4f.: 'Now Mesha king of Moab was a sheep breeder; and he had to deliver annually to the king of Israel a hundred thousand lambs, and the wool of a hundred thousand rams. But when Ahab died, the king of Moab rebelled against the king of Israel').

The language of the inscription is very close to biblical Hebrew. The identical term *ḥrm* is used (line 17).

This Moabite text is of great importance. For in view of the numerous late, purely theoretical, biblical texts on the ban it confirms that some of the biblical narratives and laws about it are realistic and historically credible. This is true even though the Mesha inscription does not simply list facts, but is also shaped by court propaganda. Thus for example the statement that Israel is destroyed for ever (line 7) is an exaggeration. Nevertheless the inscription is of incalculable value as a historical source. So anyone who says that 'there is no reliable historical evidence of the implementation of a consecration to destruction in Israel' (Fritz 1994: 72) may at first sight be making an accurate statement, but is nevertheless probably not doing justice to historical truth. For the Mesha inscription is clear indirect evidence for the use of the ban in Israel also, and by no means only a historical model on which the Old Testament narratives have orientated themselves. Moreover the parallel suggests that the practices and principles of the ban in Israel have been taken over from a background which Israel had in common with the Moabites. The Old Testament regarded the two peoples as related, since Moab is allegedly descended from Lot, Abraham's nephew (cf. Gen. 11.27; 19.37).

Is the ban historically excusable?

Since it is certain that the ban in Israel at least partly goes back to the time of the conquest of Canaan and at the same time was given literary elaboration in constantly new fictions, in the following reflections I shall keep referring simultaneously to both levels, the historical and the fictitious. Another reason why this must be allowed in the present work is because I have taken as my starting point Holy Scripture, which does not distinguish between fact and fiction, and the generalization that the Bible contains the good message of the mercy of God for all human beings.

Now the Hebrew practice of consecration to destruction can hardly be excused or trivialized by the parallel of the ban mentioned above which is directed against Israel (for this and what follows cf. Barr 1993: 209f.). To heighten the offensiveness even more: according to the Old Testament texts, the ban is not something that took place only once, that can be understood as a meaningful part of ancient anthropology, and can be used fruitfully in theological paraenesis; no, *it is something which Yahweh commanded and on which he insisted strictly.* And here immediately the ethical question arises: how can such an offensive practice be reconciled with what we traditionally regard as God?

The discussion of the Holy War in biblical theology

In what follows, by biblical theology I shall understand all those approaches which are concerned to see the Old and the New Testaments as a unity (cf. Kraus 1970). This is done with reference to the fact that 'in the two Testaments there is testimony not to two gods but to the one and only Lord' (Janowski and Welker 1986: 6) and with the aim of making specific 'how the revelation of Yahweh to Israel and that in Jesus Christ given "once for all" can be thought together and expressed theologically in our present' (ibid.). However, as is clear from a look at the publications concerned, their advocates do not touch on the question which has just been raised, and protest loudly if it is discussed at all. Doubt about the possibility of justifying the ban is always interpreted as a sign of theological liberalism or as Marcionism which undermines the authority of the Old Testament (cf. e.g. Dietrich and Link 1995: 80; for the senselessness of the charge most recently made cf. Barr 1971: 34–6, who rightly points out that in contrast to their alleged model, the present-day 'Marcionites' are driven by an affirmation of present-day life). Hence there is no discussion of this question in the more recent contributions to biblical theology which are regularly published in the new *Jahrbuch für Biblische Theologie* (since 1986) either. Evidently this is not regarded as an ethical problem or, if it does exist, biblical theology does not seem in a position to make any contribution here.

Integration of the dark side of God?

Others content themselves with investigating the experiences which 'have led to such alien texts. Why have they been allowed to stand, and why have they found a way into the canon at all? ... Our theological thought wants to purge God of all cruel, intolerant and threatening features. Only then, we think, can we hold to him as God. But precisely the opposite is the case. Perhaps only a God who takes on the extreme in alienation, pain and involvement is in a position to give hope to a world which suffers from such expectations' (Dietrich and Link 1995: 16). Quite apart from the fact that sermonic language, which has no place in an academic dissertation, finds its way in here in the 'perhaps' which is used twice, it is not at all clear that a God can give hope to the world only if he has a share in its cruelties. *Cruelty remains cruelty even if the Bible attributes it to God.* To this we must always prefer Jesus of Nazareth's picture of God, the only one that can give human beings hope: the picture of a deity who loves and does not hate, who builds up and does not destroy, who preserves life and does not extinguish it in a cold-blooded way (cf. further below, 128–130).

It is too cheap for the two authors of the quotation above to accuse the Enlightenment of having led people into perplexity and resignation (cf. ibid., Foreword). We need to look at the logic of this argument: it is suggested that at least for the time being we must flee back into the arms of a cruel God because the Enlightenment has no positive recipe for present-day humankind (a view which can only be regarded as a defamation). So I can only regard these attempts to integrate the dark sides of God as a desperate apologetic attempt. Once again, cruelty remains cruelty even if it is ordained by God in a highly personal way, and must be ruled out where God is concerned.

A current attempt to acknowledge the dark sides of God is that undertaken by Thomas Römer (1996). Here, too, the God of the Old Testament is characterized by a combination of wrath and mercy. Römer thinks it necessary to look at these two things together in order to express the different experiences which the people of Israel accumulated with its God. These contrary experiences should not allow one to narrow down the biblical God to the 'good God'. So Römer does not want to trivialize the sharpness of the passages in the Old Testament in which a tyrannical and violent God appears. Rather, he wants to make them understandable in their particular cultural and historical context. Certainly he himself repudiates some features of the Old Testament God, but he still finds hidden meaning in the very texts which he repudiates with the help of contextualization. Among other things, he even makes out in them an opposition within the Bible which is directed against the violent streaks in the picture of God. Thus for example the story of the sacrifice of Isaac (Gen. 22) is meant to be a protest against the practice of child sacrifice, also customary in Israel at times of crises which threatened existence. Over against this Abraham is emphasized as a model of faith for whom God intervenes, giving him a sacrificial animal instead of his son. The sacrifices themselves are an expression of the wrath of Yahweh (64). The divine command to Abraham to sacrifice his son remains incomprehensible, since in this way God is fighting against God.

Römer makes a similar point in connection with other texts: looked at in this way, even highly warlike texts are still understood as an expression of the sole worship of Yahweh. Their significance is grounded in the fact that they are a subversive defence against the claims of the secular authorities, for example the Assyrian kings (82). These required of their vassals, among which Israel also belonged, 'You shall love the Lord your king!' The biblical texts allow this claim only for their God. To make his authority credible, they transferred the warlike attributes of the Assyrian kings to Yahweh, so as to be able to declare him to be the stronger king and God. Even in the most warlike biblical text, the book of Joshua, Römer makes out an anti-militaristic, liberation-theological emphasis. Right at the beginning, the warrior Joshua is painted over by the later generations of the Deuteronomic school with the features of a rabbi (Josh. 1.8). Here, as also in Exodus (ch.14), the writers are concerned that God alone should fight. The success of human warlike activities is regarded with scepticism, and human beings are 'disarmed'.

Now this cannot take place without 'arming' God; but once the meaning of this is worked out, the statements about God's authoritative rule appear as a regrettable deviation. Contrary to the programme of an 'ethnic cleansing' of Israel, in the stories of Abraham we have a God of peaceful co-existence as the counterpart to an exclusive God (95). Römer explains the deviations which go so far as a warlike picture of God as the expression of a national crisis and attaches importance to the fact that the 'holy wars' and implementations of the ban did not take place, but represent an expression of the threatened national identity of Israel, bowed down by foreign rule and the pressure to assimilate.

So according to Römer, in the biblical writings themselves there is always an alternative proposal for the image of God. But he does not indicate where the dividing line runs that helps us to draw a distinction between the cruelties of the biblical God which are to be rejected and the attributes which allegedly belong to his dark side. With what right, however, should so much understanding be devoted to these texts that even today they are meaningful for the Christian faith and the question of suffering, over and above their historical relevance?

Römer ends his argument by asserting that in the Bible we

stand over against an incomprehensible liberator God (118). This God is to be allowed the freedom to have compassion on whom he will. But this very construction of a liberator God is in question. What else can the aim of a comprehensive liberation be if not the end of violence, oppression and concealment? So why should not criteria corresponding to human action apply to the divine action, on an equal footing? If one attributes total freedom and complete otherness to God, one easily overlooks the fact that the transcendental reality of God which goes beyond us is far more human than the idea of the supernatural character of God may allow. Since Römer's construction within the Bible cannot raise these questions, there is no avoiding a split between on the one hand taking brutal biblical texts seriously and on the other their deliberate reinterpretation. So Römer finally withdraws into an alleged paradox in faith.

The unity of the divine anger and the divine mercy is also said to have been revealed in the violent sacrificial death of Jesus (75). Precisely here Römer leaves his previous hermeneutical approach by significantly no longer citing any opposing Christian and Jewish texts. Römer's superficial openness to questioning violent divine action leaves modern men and women where they are encountered: in their dismay that loving mercy and naked power are to be united in God, whether visibly or secretly.

Reasons for the slaughter of the Canaanites

How was the slaughter of the Canaanites justified theologically?

One traditional answer runs that the Canaanites had been extremely wicked. In this connection I shall go on to quote at rather greater length than usual, as I have already done once (see above 11), from the work of a forgotten theologian, Hermann Samuel Reimarus (1694–1768), who deliberately did not publish it during his lifetime. He thought that his contemporaries would not be able to accept the historical insights that he had gained, for want of sufficient enlightenment.

Reimarus's observations on the Old Testament are largely due to his preoccupation with the English deists (cf. Reventlow 1985), chief among them Thomas Morgan (1680–1743), 'who branded the Old Testament the document of a narrow-minded nationalistic Jewish religion' (Gunneweg 1978: 150), but also pointed out many historical and substantive causes of offence which have still to be removed.

Gotthold Ephraim Lessing (1729–1781) published fragments of the New Testament part of Reimarus's book after his death, thereby sparking off a controversy which is still alive today. Now, as the whole of Hermann Samuel Reimarus' book entitled *Apologia or Defence for the Rational Worshippers of God* has been available since 1972, this honest Hamburg scholar should at least find more of a hearing in the present.

On the view that the Canaanites were morally inferior and therefore had to be exterminated he wrote:

> Listen to the way in which our theological gentlemen excuse the actions of Joshua. They say that the Canaanites were wicked people, given over to idolatry and all the unnatural sins of fleshly lusts. And as they had fulfilled the measure of their sins, the just God wanted to look on their wickedness no longer but to know that they had been eradicated from the earth. Indeed he is Lord of people's lives and goods, and no one will accuse him of injustice if he has even the most extreme punishments meted out to such wicked people, and gives their whole land and all their possessions to others. Now that was the cause of the procedure which seems harsh. God enjoined his people, the Israelites, at the same time to be his judges, and they were to spare no one, so that they would never be led astray to such abominations by the Canaanites; and therefore he had promised them so to speak all the confiscated property as their possession. Now just as an executioner does not become a murderer by killing criminals on the orders of the ruler, nor a servant of the court become a robber by confiscating and appropriating goods given to him, so too Joshua and the Israelites must be judged from this

perspective. What would not have been allowed to other peoples and would have been highly criminal was not only allowed to the Israelites but was even their duty.

So the mitigation of the otherwise unjust and cruel treatment of the Canaanites depends on a direct command of God and on blaming them for the crimes of which they were guilty. The miraculous help which God is said to have given Joshua in the conquest of Jericho and at other times must then serve as a proof of the divine command. But we do not find evidence for such penal crimes on the part of the Canaanites except in the accusation of Moses and the historian (Reimarus, 1972a: 481f.).

Truly, the degree of wickedness of the Canaanites is only legendary and has probably been invented to justify the extreme cruelty of the mass exterminations reported by the biblical text. And while even within the Old Testament the Canaanites are often depicted as abominable, that may usually be due to the fact that the Israelites had become alienated from the Canaanites and therefore attributed all kinds of wickednesses to their opponents. Where detailed contacts with the Canaanites and other non-Hebrew peoples are depicted, the remarks are relatively sympathetic (cf. Gen.34) and do not suggest extreme wickedness. Of course some religious aberrations were attributed during the monarchy to the imitation of Canaanite customs (II Kings 16.3; 23.10). The sacrifices of children mentioned there were forbidden by laws in Israel. That shows that they also in fact occurred there. But the slaughter of the whole population of Canaan including the children, whose sacrifice was regarded as abominable, is a remarkable way of overcoming the practice of child sacrifice. Fearful as the sacrifices of children are, they provide no excuse for exterminating the Canaanite population in its entirety. Moreover apart from this practice there is no evidence of unusual wickedness within Canaanite culture.

At no time can there be different opinions on genocide

Ethical misconduct, however great it may be, never justifies genocide. Now these massacres were by no means ordered because of the moral inferiority of the population but for other reasons. The Canaanites were exterminated because they lived in the land which Israel was to inhabit in accordance with the will of its God Yahweh. If the people of God needed its own land, why were the inhabitants of the cities concerned not offered emigration, instead of – as has been said – being slaughtered?

But should not the historical conditioning of Israel's way of waging war deter us from a radical condemnation? The theological view lurking behind this question evidently assumes that genocide, which is to be repudiated in the present-day modern world, was perhaps acceptable to an earlier period or is relativized by comparison with the cruelties of which modern men are increasingly capable. All that is weak and apologetic. In the face of a deliberate obliteration of whole populations by order of God there is no room for different opinions – either at that time or in our century, in which ugly examples of genocide have taken place (for the above cf. Barr 1993: 217).

The fact remains: the command to exterminate is extremely offensive, even if at that time it was given by God in a highly personal way; or, more precisely, even if people at that time believed that God was ordering extermination. Anyone who accuses me at this point of unhistorical thinking ('one cannot measure an alien time by modern standards') is asked to imagine the acts performed at the ban and their consequences, and to think through in detail what crimes were really perpetrated here: the deliberate slaughter of infants, children, women and men. Only then will they also understand the emotional aspect of my question how such acts can still have anything to do with the mercy of God and why the biblical theologians can so quickly pass over from such a crime against humanity allegedly ordained by God to the order of the day.

C. The election of Israel and its consequences for others

Deuteronomy and its message

The key word 'elect' or 'chosen' appears regularly in the context of the texts on the ban cited above. In the book of Deuteronomy (= second law) derived from a (wrong) Greek translation of Deut. 17.18, which really speaks of a copy of the law, this connection comes out particularly clearly. The verb 'choose' is a favourite one for this book, which uses it 30 times (compared with 153 times in the whole of the Old Testament).

Old Testament scholars with the most varied views emphasize the significance of Deuteronomy in a positive way, as the following three views may indicate.

'The special feature of Deuteronomy is that here an entire legislative code is set within the sphere of immense hope and expectation. God's demand on the people does not stand there in a timeless way but is illuminated by the promise that new hope is to be disclosed to Israel. A people empowered with a great hope is here called on to be obedient to the commandments' (Zimmerli 1971: 74).

'Deuteronomy is a theological book. There is probably no other book in the Old Testament of which this could be said so clearly. It outlines an overall view of Israel's faith in the one God and in the unique relationship of this God to the people whom he has chosen; such a view did not exist before or after. This outline is intrinsically very consistent' (Rendtorff 1985: 155).

'In every respect Deuteronomy forms the centre of the Old Testament. Thanks to its setting in the late seventh century, in time and content it represents the focal point for the literature and religious history of the Old Testament. By its influence on the work of the Deuteronomistic school it persistently governed the understanding of the history and prophecy of Israel. The significance of Deuteronomy for the further history of Judaism and also Christianity and Islam can hardly be overestimated' (Kaiser 1992: 91).

Content

Deuteronomy is predominantly stylized as a farewell discourse of Moses to Israel which he gives at the end of the wandering in the wilderness before the crossing of the Jordan. Its centre is the Deuteronomistic law in Deut. 12–26. What comes before and after is relatively disparate and diffuse. We are struck by the frequent change between singular and plural in the form of address, and the repetition of Deut. 6.6–9 in Deut. 11.18–20. From this follows the compelling conclusion that chs.12–26 cannot have been composed from the start as a literary whole. However, the framework (chs.1–11 and 27–33) displays a relatively unitary structure in both language and content (cf. the three views quoted above and the detailed analysis).

Scholars do not agree about how to demarcate the various strata. Following Martin Noth, I would assume that Deut. 1.1–4.43 and Deut 31–34 have been added to Deuteronomy later, and that therefore Deut. 4.44–30.20 contains the original Deuteronomy (cf. Noth 1963: 14).

Detailed analysis

Chapters 6–11 contain several liturgical formulations for celebrating the presentation of the law. However, the edges of the units are often blurred, and the whole passage, which has now become literature as a fictitious speech of Moses, has been removed from its original setting in the practical cultic sphere (cf. von Rad 1953: 40f.).

Deut. 7.6–8 states: '6 For you are a people holy to Yahweh your God; Yahweh your God has *chosen* you to be a people for his own possession, out of all the peoples that are on the face of the earth. 7 It was not because you were more in number than any other people that Yahweh set his love upon you and *chose* you, for you were the fewest of all peoples; 8 but it is because Yahweh loves you, and is keeping the oath which he swore to your fathers, that Yahweh has brought you out with a mighty hand, and redeemed you from the house of bondage, from the hand of Pharaoh king of Egypt.'

It should be noted that in the immediate context of this passage it is said: '1 When Yahweh your God brings you into the land which you are entering to take possession of it, and clears away many nations before you... greater and mightier than your-selves, 2 and when Yahweh your God gives them over to you, and you defeat them; then you must utterly destroy them; you shall make no covenant with them, and show no mercy to them' (Deut. 7.1–2).

There is a similar definition of the relationship between the extermination of the inhabitants of Canaan and the election of Israel in Deut. 9.1–5:

1 Hear, O Israel; you are to pass over the Jordan this day, to go in to dispossess nations greater and mightier than your-selves, cities great and fortified up to heaven, 2 a people great and tall, the sons of the Anakim, whom you know, and of whom you have heard it said, 'Who can stand before the sons of Anak?' 3 Know therefore this day that he who goes over before you as a devouring fire is Yahweh your God; he will destroy them and subdue them before you; so you shall drive them out, and make them perish quickly, as the Lord has promised you. 4 Do not say in your heart, after Yahweh your God has thrust them out before you, 'It is because of my righteousness that Yahweh has brought me in to possess this land'; whereas it is because of the wickedness of these nations that Yahweh is driving them out before you. 5 Not because of your righteousness or the uprightness of your heart are you going in to possess their land; but because of the wickedness of these nations Yahweh your God is driving them out from

before you, and that he may confirm the word which Yahweh
swore to your fathers, to Abraham, to Isaac, and to Jacob.

Granted, the explicit expression 'choose' does not occur here,
but it is doubtless presupposed. So the intervention of Yahweh
for Israel is motivated by the evil of the peoples *and* the word
that he has sworn to Abraham, Isaac and Jacob. Cf. similarly
Deut. 7.8: because Yahweh loves his people and wants to keep
the oath which he has made to the fathers, he has chosen his
people. Note also the similarity between Deut. 8 and Deut. 9.
Both chapters report the generous action of Yahweh towards
Israel. He leads it into the fertile land (8.7f.; 9.1) and destroys
its enemies (8.20; 9.3). At the same time the possibility of Israel
ascribing Yahweh's glorious acts to itself is firmly ruled out
(8.17; 9.4). Both units emphasize the covenant with the patriarchs and thus in fact the election of Israel.

According to the texts quoted above, the future of the people
consists in being given a rich land by Yahweh. This also
includes the centralization of its worship. The reason for this is
given as follows: '8 You shall not do according to all that we are
doing here this day, every man doing whatever is right in his
own eyes; 9 for you have not as yet come to the rest and the
inheritance which Yahweh your God gives you. 10 But you will
go over the Jordan, and live in the land which Yahweh your
God gives you to inherit, and he will give you rest from all your
enemies round about, so that you live in safety.' Then Yahweh
makes rest for Israel before its enemies: 'Therefore when
Yahweh your God has given you rest from all your enemies
round about, in the land which the Lord your God gives you for
an inheritance to possess, you shall blot out the remembrance of
Amalek from under heaven; you shall not forget' (Deut. 25.19).

Israel has become the holy people for Yahweh, so that the
surrounding peoples will fear it: 'Yahweh will establish you as
a people holy to himself, as he has sworn to you, if you keep the
commandments of the Lord your God and walk in his ways.
And all the peoples of the earth shall see that you are called by
the name of the Lord; and they shall be afraid of you' (Deut.

28.9–10). However, at present Israel has 'not as yet come to the rest and to the inheritance' (Deut. 12.9).

What kind of a time was it in which the problems of the present were cloaked by the past before the existence of the state and in which Deuteronomy undertook that unprece-- dented updating of the time of Moses? In what circles was Deuteronomy composed? How did its authors attempt to turn back the wheel of history? And how does Deuteronomy understand the Holy War to which it issues a call, but which must really have taken place half a millennium previously?

Only a historical analysis can shed light on this and help us to a better understanding of the purpose of Deuteronomy.

Deuteronomy and its 'discovery' under Josiah

A stroke of luck for scholars is that in all probability the report of the discovery of Deuteronomy has been preserved. The text relating to it runs as follows:

II Kings 22.1–23.24

22.1 Josiah was eight years old when he began to reign, and he reigned thirty-one years in Jerusalem ...

3 In the eighteenth year of King Josiah, the king sent Shaphan the son of Azaliah, son of Meshullam, the secretary, to the house of Yahweh, saying, 4 'Go up to Hilkiah the high priest, that he may reckon the amount of the money which has been brought into the house of Yahweh, which the keepers of the threshold have collected from the people ...'

8 And Hilkiah the high priest said to Shaphan the secretary, 'I have found the book of the law in the house of Yahweh.' And Hilkiah gave the book to Shaphan, and he read it ... 10 Then Shaphan the secretary told the king, 'Hildah the priest has given me a book.' And Shaphan read it before the king. 11 And when the king heard the words of the book of the law, he rent his clothes. 12 And the king commanded ... saying, 'Go, inquire of Yahweh for me, and

for the people, and for all Judah, concerning the words of this book that has been found; for great is the wrath of Yahweh that is kindled against us, because our fathers have not obeyed the words of this book, to do according to all that is written concerning us.'

14 So Hilkiah the priest, and Ahikam, and Achbor, and Shaphan, and Asaiah went to Huldah the prophetess ... and they talked with her. 15 And she said to them ... 18 'But as to the king of Judah, who sent you to inquire of Yahweh, thus shall you say to him, Thus says Yahweh, the God of Israel: Regarding the words which you have heard, 19 because your heart was penitent, and you humbled yourself before Yahweh, when you heard how I spoke against this place, and against its inhabitants, that they should become a desolation and a curse, and you have rent your clothes and wept before me, I also have heard you, says Yahweh. 20 Therefore, behold, I will gather you to your fathers, and you shall be gathered to your grave in peace, and your eyes shall not see all the evil which I will bring upon this place.' And they brought back word to the king.

23.1 Then the king sent, and all the elders of Judah and Jerusalem were gathered to him. 2 And the king went up to the house of Yahweh, and with him all the men of Judah and all the inhabitants of Jerusalem, and the priests and the prophets, all the people, both small and great; and he read in their hearing all the words of the book of the covenant which had been found in the house of Yahweh. 3 And the king stood by the pillar and made a covenant before Yahweh, to walk after Yahweh and to keep his commandments and his testimonies and his statutes, with all his heart and all his soul, to perform the words of this covenant that were written in this book; and all the people joined in the covenant.

4 And the king commanded Hilkiah, the high priest, and the priests of the second order, and the keepers of the threshold, to bring out of the temple of Yahweh all the vessels made for Baal, for Asherah, and for all the host of heaven; he burned them outside Jerusalem in the fields of the

Kidron, and carried their ashes to Bethel. 5 And he deposed the idolatrous priests whom the kings of Judah had ordained to burn incense in the high places at the cities of Judah and round about Jerusalem; those also who burned incense to Baal, to the sun, and the moon, and the constellations, and all the host of the heavens. 6 And he brought out the Asherah from the house of Yahweh, outside Jerusalem, to the brook Kidron, and burned it at the brook Kidron, and beat it to dust and cast the dust of it upon the graves of the common people. 7 And he broke down the houses of the male cult prostitutes which were in the house of Yahweh, where the women wove hangings for the Asherah. 8 And he brought all the priests out of the cities of Judah, and defiled the high places where the priests had burned incense, from Geba to Beersheba; and he broke down the high places of the gates that were at the entrance of Joshua the governor of the city, which were on one's left at the gate of the city. 9 However, the priests of the high places did not come up to the altar of Yahweh in Jerusalem, but they ate unleavened bread among their brethren. 10 And he defiled Topheth, which is in the valley of the sons of Hinnom, that no one might burn his son or his daughter as an offering to Molech. 11 And he removed the horses that the kings of Judah had dedicated to the sun, at the entrance to the house of Yahweh, by the chamber of Nathan-melech the chamberlain, which was in the precincts; and he burned the chariots of the sun with fire. 12 And the altars on the roof of the upper chamber of Ahaz, which the kings of Judah had made, and the altars which Manasseh had made in the two courts of the house of Yahweh, he pulled down and broke in pieces, and cast the dust of them into the brook Kidron. And the king defiled the high places that were east of Jerusalem, to the south of the mount of corruption, which Solomon the king of Israel had built for Ashtoreth the abomination of the Sidonians, and for Chemosh the abomination of Moab, and for Milcom the abomination of the Ammonites. 14 And he broke in pieces the pillars, and cut down the Asherim, and filled their places with the bones of men.

15 Moreover the altar at Bethel, the high place erected by Jeroboam the son of Nebat, who made Israel to sin, that altar with the high place he pulled down and he broke in pieces its stones, crushing them to dust; also he burned the Asherah. 16 And as Josiah turned, he saw the tombs there on the mount; and he sent and took the bones out of the tombs, and burned them upon the altar, and defiled it, according to the word of Yahweh which the man of God proclaimed, who had predicted these things. 17 Then he said, 'What is yonder monument that I see?' And the men of the city told him, 'It is the tomb of the man of God who came from Judah and predicted these things which you have done against the altar at Bethel.' 18 And he said, 'Let him be; let no man move his bones.' So they let his bones alone, with the bones of the prophet who came out of Samaria.

19 And all the shrines also of the high places that were in the cities of Samaria, which kings of Israel had made, provoking Yahweh to anger, Josiah removed; he did to them according to all that he had done at Bethel. 20 And he slew all the priests of the high places who were there, upon the altars, and burned the bones of men upon them. Then he returned to Jerusalem.

21 And the king commanded all the people, 'Keep the passover to Yahweh your God, as it is written in this book of the covenant.' 22 For no such passover had been kept since the days of the judges who judged Israel, or during all the days of the kings of Israel or of the kings of Judah; 23 but in the eighteenth year of King Josiah this passover was kept to Yahweh.

24 Moreover Josiah put away the mediums and the wizards and the teraphim and the idols and all the abominations that were seen in the land of Judah and in Jerusalem, that he might establish the words of the law which were written in the book that Hilkiah the priest found in the house of the Lord.

Anyone who reads this text will regard the law described here as historical until proven otherwise and therefore look for the existence of the book (for what follows see Smend 1989, 76f.).

The most important indication of the identity of the book of the law with Deuteronomy lies in the parallel between the main measures of the king and the regulations in Deuteronomy:

	II Kings	Deut.
Removal of		
– the asherahs (= the wooden poles which went with the cult of the goddess Asherah)	23.4, 6f., 14	12.3;16.21
– star worship	23.4f., 11	17.3
– temple prostitution	23.7	23.18
– the sanctuaries outside the capital ('high places') and the alien cults	23.8, 13, 15, 19f.	12f.
– child sacrifice	23.10	12.31;18.10
– the mazzeboth (= cultic stones)	23.14	12.3; 16.22
– conjuring up the dead	23.24	18.11
Passover in Jerusalem	23.21–23	16.1–8

Two further arguments support the historical plausibility of the narrative. First, the normative character which the Deuteronomic law has in the Deuteronomic History, to which II Kings 22f. in fact belongs. Secondly, the report in II Kings 22f. with the king as the central figure; the enquiry made of the prophetess Huldah, who is otherwise unknown; the appointment of high officials, sometimes known only before the exile, to perform particular tasks; and the involvement of the elders of Judah and Jerusalem (cf. Spieckermann 1982: 155ff.).

Granted, we cannot think here of the whole of Deuteronomy in its present form, since chs.1–3 (4) and 31–34 are secondary additions. Moreover it is extremely probable that further additions were also made after the exile. But none of this can alter the fact that the original form of Deuteronomy is to be identified with the book found under Josiah. In that case 622 BCE would be the *terminus ante quem* for the composition of the book.

There may have been even earlier forms of Deuteronomy, but I shall leave them out of account, as I shall leave out of account the later additions. Historically this means that in 622 the Jerusalem priesthood passed on a lawbook to the king. Through the discovery of the book, Deuteronomy found its way into the hands of King Josiah. He recognized the importance of its content for reshaping Yahweh religion and also the necessary political consequences. In view of the radical nature of the political and theological demands of Deuteronomy it is remarkable that Josiah so rapidly declared himself in agreement with them and immediately put them into practice. This may be because (like Joash earlier, cf. II Kings 12.3) he had been brought up by priests to whom Deuteronomic thought was familiar. In that case he would not have heard the Deuteronomic law for the first time in the eighteenth year of his reign, though he will have read it for the first time then (cf. Spieckermann 1982: 379).

However, it is with these observations that the historical questions first begin. Was the original form of Deuteronomy really 'found', or was the history of its discovery just invented? Granted, today Old Testament theologians reject the possibility of pious fraud. According to Spieckermann the timing and the narrative tell against this, as does the good theological insight which underlies Deuteronomy (cf. Spieckermann 1982: 156f.). But these reasons are no alternative to pious deception. For even a deceiver can be guided by honourable theological motives. (Whether this is *still* credible *today* is another question.) In that case the important question is whether there were similar 'events' of discovering books in antiquity which help us better to understand this 'discovery' under Josiah. 'Similar events explain one another and a comparison between them leads to a deeper understanding of the individual instance. To grasp this in its historical character always remains the last task of history ' (Meyer 1912: 12; cf. Speyer 1970: 145f.).

I shall therefore go on to present and investigate two ancient accounts of discoveries and one modern one. In advance I should emphasize that many more could be added from both pagan (cf. Leipoldt and Morenz 1953: 28f.) and Christian (cf. Speyer 1971: 68) antiquity.

The rediscovered books of King Numa

The discovery of the books of King Numa, the legendary second king of Rome, in 181 BCE, is the earliest in Roman history. The original account of it can be gained from a variety of writers. I shall give it in the versions, first of Pliny the Elder (23/24–79 CE), transcribing several earlier authors whom he mentions by name, and then of the church father Augustine, which goes back to Varro (born 116 BCE). The versions in Livy (40, 29, 3–14) and Plutarch (*Numa* 22) can be left out of account here.

Pliny, *Natural History* 13, 84–87: 'Cassius Hermina, a historian of great antiquity [middle of the second century BCE], had stated in his *Annals* Book IV that the secretary Gnaeus Terentius, when digging over his land on the Janicula, turned up a coffer that had contained the body of Numa, who was king of Rome, and that in the same coffer were found some books of his – this was in the consulship of Publius Cornelius Cethegus, son of Lucius, and of Marcus Baebius Tamphilus, son of Quintus [i.e. 181 BCE], dating 535 years after the accession of Numa. And the historian says that the books were made of paper, which makes the matter even more remarkable, because of their having lasted in a hole in the ground, and consequently a point of such importance I will quote in the words of Hermina himself: Other people wondered how those books could have lasted so long, but Terentius's explanation was that about in the middle of the coffer there had been a square stone tied all around with wax cords, and that the three books had been placed on the top of this stone: and he thought that this position was the reason why they had not decayed; and that the books had been soaked in citrus oil, and he thought that this was why they were not moth-eaten. These books contained the philosophical doctrines of Pythagoras, and Hermina said that the book had been burnt by the Praetor Quintus Petulius because they were writings of philosophy. The same story is recorded by Piso the former censor in his commentaries, Book I, but he says that there were seven volumes of pontifical law and the same number of Pythagorean philosophy: while Tuditanus in Book XIII says that there were twelve volumes of the *Decrees of Numa*; Varro himself says that there were seven volumes of *Antiquities of Man*, and Antias in his second book speaks of there having been twelve volumes *On Matters Pontifical* written in Latin and the same number in Greek containing *Doctrines of Philosophy*. Antias also quotes in Book III a Resolution of the Senate deciding that these volumes were to be burnt.'

Augustine, *City of God*, VII, 34: Varro writes in his book on the cult of the gods: 'A certain Terentius had some ground near to Mount Janiculum; and as his servants were ploughing near to Numa's tomb, the plough turned up some books containing the ceremonies' institutions. Terentius brought them into the city to the praetor, who having looked in them, brought this so weighty an affair before the Senate: where having read some of the first causes why he had instituted this and that in their religion, the senate agreed with dead Numa, and like religious fathers, gave order to the praetor for the burning of them.'

In antiquity no one doubted the fact of the discovery. But the claim that Numa had been a disciple of Pythagoras was rejected. Nowadays the books discovered at that time are regarded as 'forgeries by Neopythagorean circles ... A condition for their composition was the revived enthusiasm for Pythagoras and his school' (Speyer 1970: 54; cf. also Zeller 1963: 92–174, esp. 99–103, who relativizes the Neopythagorean origin of the books). Here too the universal law applies: 'Any party tends to attribute its pseudonymous writings to such authors as are regarded as an authority by themselves and the readers for whom these are first intended, and therefore preferably its founder: the Orphics Orpheus and the Pythagoreans Pythagoras' (Zeller 1963: 102).

The rediscovered books of Alexander of Abonuteichos

Lucian of Samosata (born c.120 CE) writes in his work *Alexander the False Prophet* that Alexander and his companion Coconnas went to Chalcedon 'and in the age-old temple of Apollo there dug up some iron tablets with an inscription which stated that Aesculapius would very soon come to Pontus with his father Apollo and take up his abode in Abonuteichos. These tablets were carefully arranged in such a way that they had to be found, and so the story of them quickly spread through Bithynia and in all Pontus; and in Abonuteichos, where they were first brought, the inhabitants decided without delay to build a temple and really began to dig a foundation.'

Lucian's tractate is a polemic against Alexander, whose practices were aimed at increasing popular belief in miracles and thus at reinforcing belief in his own person. The digging up of tablets related in the above text hardly derives from Lucian's polemic and is credible. At the same time it puts Alexander's character in the right light and makes his action seem shady.

The discovery of The Book of Mormon by Joseph Smith

The most momentous discovery of a book in modern times is without doubt that of The Book of Mormon by Joseph Smith (1805–1844). Smith composed an account of how he came into possession of The Book of Mormon, the main points of which are printed in all editions of The Book of Mormon. Here are the most important extracts:

> While I was thus in the act of calling upon God, I discovered a light appearing in my room, which continued to increase until the room was lighter than at noonday, when immediately a personage appeared at my bedside, standing in the air, for his feet did not touch the floor ...
>
> He called me by name, and said unto me that he was a messenger sent from the presence of God to me, and that his name was Moroni; that God had a work for me to do; and that my name should be had for good and evil among all

nations, kindreds, and tongues, or that it should be both good and evil spoken of among all people.

He said there was a book deposited, written upon gold plates, giving an account of the former inhabitants of this continent, and the source from whence they sprang. He also said that the fullness of the everlasting Gospel was contained in it, as delivered by the Saviour to the ancient inhabitants;

Also, that there were two stones in silver bows – and these stones, fastened to a breastplate, constituted what is called the Urim and Thummim – deposited with the plates; and the possession and use of these stones were what constituted Seers in ancient or former times; and that God had prepared them for the purpose of translating the book.

Again, he told me, that when I got those plates of which he had spoken – for the time that they should be obtained was not yet fulfilled – I should not show them to any person; neither the breastplate with the Urim and Thummim; only to those to whom I should be commanded to show them; if I did I should be destroyed. While he was conversing with me about the plates, the vision was opened to my mind that I could see the place where the plates were deposited, and that so clearly and distinctly that I knew the place again when I visited it ...

At length the time arrived for obtaining the plates, the Urim and Thummim, and the breastplate. On the twenty-second day of September, one thousand eight hundred and twenty-seven, having gone as usual at the end of another year to the place where they were deposited, the same heavenly messenger delivered them up to me with this charge: That I should be responsible for them; that if I should let them go carelessly, or through any neglect of mine, I should be cut off; but that if I would use all my endeavours to preserve them, until he, the messenger, should call for them, they should be protected.

I soon found out the reason why I had received such strict charges to keep them safe, and why it was that the messenger had said that when I had done what was required at my hand, he would call for them. For no sooner was it known that I had them, than the most strenuous exertions were used to get them from me. Every stratagem that could be invented was resorted to for that purpose. The persecution became more bitter and severe than before, and multitudes were on the alert continually to get them from me if possible. But by the wisdom of God, they remained safe in my hands, until I had accomplished by them what was required at my hand. When, according to arrangements, the messenger called for them, I delivered them up to him; and he has them in his charge until this day, being the second day of May, one thousand eight hundred and thirty-eight.

It is impossible to doubt the authenticity of Joseph Smith's experience. He is a prophet and the founder of a religion. As the work of the ancient historian Eduard Meyer (1912) has shown, we must grant Joseph Smith the subjective belief that he was inspired by God. Like Christianity, the movement which he founded, the percentage increase in whose members exceeds that of all other Christian churches, knows visions, miraculous healings and speaking with tongues in its initial period. Smith's influence on those around him and the history of the Mormon church also make one doubt that the movement began exclusively from blatant deceit.

Certainly Christian theologians have often spoken of 'total forgery' in connection with The Book of Mormon. 'Underlying The Book of Mormon is ... a historical construction (viz. of the Israelites who emigrated to America). This is a *construction,* i.e. a depiction of what the course of history had to be. To put it another way: in this book the ideals of the present are projected back on to history, and its course is depicted as it really should have taken place in accordance with these ideals' (Meinhold 1962: 576). But formally speaking, this judgment also applies to Deuteronomy, which was composed more than 600 years after the events it describes, and for example also to the Acts of the Apostles (cf. Lüdemann 1989), although that is far closer to actual history than The Book of Mormon and Deuteronomy. So

Peter Meinhold's judgment is unjust and overlooks the fact that authentic religion must always offer artificial historical constructions, since our experience is that reality and religious conviction are always in tension with each other.

Forgery or authentic religious pseudepigraphy?

The leading expert on pseudepigraphy (= false attribution) today, Wolfgang Speyer, has introduced the concept of 'authentic religious pseudepigraphy' to distinguish a particular kind of pseudepigraphy, which came into being as it were under pressure from above – one thinks of the apocalyptists and certain oracles – from falsehood and literary invention. He argues that the deciding factor as to whether we have 'authentic religious pseudepigraphy' or a forgery in the guise of a religious pseudepigraphon is not its literary or religious-ethical content. Rather, the important thing is whether the author believed when writing his literary work that he had acted merely as the instrument of his God or, for whatever reasons, simply wanted to deceive (cf. Speyer 1977: 234–46).

On this basis, of the three parallels to Deuteronomy discussed above, the tablets of Alexander of Abonuteichos fall into the category of forgery and Joseph Smith's plates into that of authentic religious pseudepigraphy, while the books of Numa cannot be assigned a certain place. Here both categories are possible.

Deuteronomy as a utopia of authentic religious pseudepigraphy?

Now to which category is Deuteronomy to be assigned? I have already said that its content points to a basic theoretical programme which was worked out carefully by a group of Jerusalem priests. Furthermore, we can conjecture a certain degree of influence from the 'people of the land' who had elevated Josiah to the throne at the age of eight (II Kings 21.23f.). 'This was a middle class among the land-owning farmers of

Judah which became politically active' (Albertz 1994: 201). But parts of the aristocratic groups who had a training in wisdom, like Shaphan and the circle of scribes around him, also stand behind the Deuteronomic reform. This does not go back to a spontaneous revelation, but has been developed in careful theological work. Its authors regard themselves as instruments of God. Now if that is the case, Deuteronomy is to be regarded as *authentic religious pseudepigraphy*. To increase respect for Deuteronomy, its authors either 'planted' it in the temple so that it should be found there, or merely claimed that it had been found. To this procedure we may apply what Friedrich Nietzsche said on the phenomenon of forgery: '"I did that," says my memory. "I could not have done that," says my pride, and remains inexorable. Eventually the memory yields' (*Beyond Good and Evil*, 68).

Accordingly, this authentic religious pseudepigraphy of Deuteronomy is a utopia fabricated by several groups in Judah, a utopia which among other things calls not only for a strict centralization but also and above all for purity of the cult and for rigorous demarcation from other peoples. As Israel is the holy people, chosen by Yahweh, it must totally avoid contact with other peoples; political neutrality and religious tolerance are excluded. 'Thus the Deuteronomistic programme of separation is not just a singular deviation, but the core of a theology' (Perlitt 1972: 56). The effort to maintain the special existence of Israel and to protect it from foreign influences at any price almost necessarily produced a warlike ideology which could also adopt the age-old commandment of the ban. So it is not surprising that when Deuteronomy received the status of an official state theology under Josiah, this ideology actually resulted in military actions. Thus King Josiah made an attempt to restore the kingdom of David once again by conquering the Northern Kingdom (Perlitt 1972: 51). However, these high-flying plans proved abortive, because Josiah was killed in Megiddo in 609.

Coupled with the ideas of the unity and purity of the cult is the doctrine of election, which sought to overcome the class conflicts in the society of Judah and which had 'explicitly humane features' (Albertz 1992: 223), in that from then on groups without land were provided for on a regular basis (cf. Deut. 14.28f.; 26.12f.; the tithe is to remain in the locality every third year and at that time not be delivered to the central sanctuary, as was otherwise customary). However, outwardly segregation prevailed, along with a hatred, expressed in ritual, of everything that was not part of Israel.

The ideology of separation was further developed intellectually in the exile (587–539 BCE) and in the post-exilic period, and consistently turned against all those who did not belong to the pure cultic community. The extermination of the Canaanites which was brought about in people's minds was rooted in it, as for example is Psalm 137, which was composed in the Babylonian exile (cf. v.1: 'By the waters of Babylon, there we sat down and wept ...') and calls for vengeance: '8 O daughter of Babylon, you devastator! Happy shall he be who requites you with what you have done to us! 9 Happy shall he be who takes your little ones and dashes them against the rock!'

A recent commentator, Hans-Joachim Kraus, sees in v.9 only an 'indication of the cruelty of the actions in ancient warfare ... The call for vengeance is an appeal to the power of Yahewh in history ... in the midst of historical life it has to be decided whether Yahweh is God or whether the great powers will triumph' (Krauss 1966: 907f.). This exegesis is an example of the way in which inconvenient texts are neutralized historically and theologically. The exegesis of the church father Augustine is more original but equally untenable. He writes: 'Who are the children of Babylon? The budding bad desires. For they fight with the old desires. For when evil desire arises, before evil custom gains power over you, if the desire is still little it should in no way take on the power of a bad habit; when they are still small, shatter the desires. Are you afraid that when shattered they will not die? Dash them against the rock! And the rock was Christ' (CCL 40, 1978, 31–37). Here Augustine refers the children of Babylon allegorically to the budding bad desires which are to be shattered against the rock of Christ, to be understood allegorically, and thus provides another curious example of the 'edifying' way in which the Old Testament was dealt with in the early church.

Utopias of violence

The Holy War, which in most cases was only longed for and not waged, and the message of Deuteronomy, are loaded with violence, and those responsible for them wanted in their minds to exterminate whole peoples in the name of God. The phenomena mentioned are only the shell around a glowing kernel. Its content is the claim to exclusiveness made by an intolerant deity or, more precisely, the image of an intolerant God who chooses Israel and for better or for worse has sworn an oath with this people.

The visions of violence associated with this had devastating consequences in subsequent centuries of Jewish history, and indeed right down to the present day.

Along this line, in the post-exilic period the Book of Ezra depicts and justifies the dissolution of mixed marriages (for the details see the contribution by Kittel 1943, esp. 34–36, an article which has rightly fallen into disrepute [see below 75], but which is historically valuable). It has to happen because the natural tie with heathen sexual partners represents a breach of loyalty to Yahweh (Ezra 10.10) and thus a danger to the holiness of the elect people of God. The book of Ezra painfully lists in detail those who had taken alien wives (Ezra 10.18–43). In summary, v.44a says that all those mentioned previously were guilty of this transgression, and in its original version v.44b reports the dismissal of the wives and the children who had been born to them.

The text, which stands in the standard editions of the Hebrew Bible, literally reads: 'And there were among them women who had brought forth sons (into the world).' However, as the whole chapter is focussed on the fact that women and children were rejected (cf. vv.3, 8, 19), we are forced to assume that the text cited is not original. The explanation of this is probably the lack of success of Ezra's action. Therefore later copyists who knew about this altered the text accordingly. At the same time, did they want to indicate by this that sons might not be cast out? Thus the resistance against Ezra shows a ray of humanity which prevailed against a theologically motivated dismissal of wife and child. However, as the whole of ch.10 shows, initially the theological zealot Ezra had some success. To some degree he was continuing the Holy War into the families (cf. already Deut. 23.3: 'No one of mixed descent shall enter the assembly of Yahweh; even to the tenth generation none belonging to them shall enter the assembly of Yahweh for ever').

In view of the harshness of the regulation about mixed marriage it is sometimes conjectured with reference to the book of Ruth (the foreigner Ruth finds a home in Israel), and to the frequent instances of women coming over to Judaism, that Ezra 'wanted to break up only those marriages where the woman had not come over to Yahweh faith' (Stiegler 1994: 155). However, this harmonizing solution has no support in the text (cf. Blenkinsopp 1988: 201f.).

The pernicious long-term effect of the utopias of violence

The most pernicious consequence of the utopias of violence in the Old Testament which are bound up with the Holy War is that in the history of Christian influence, from the Crusades to the Holocaust, they were turned against the people in whose tradition they were produced.

In terms of its effect, the marriage legislation under Ezra and Nehemiah is sometimes regarded as carefully planned suicide. For antisemitism has a grotesque mirror image in the Old Testament itself. The correct insight here is that the measures taken against heathen wives (and the children of mixed marriage) show an analogy to the steps that were later introduced against Jews. As early as the Synod of Elvira (300/313 CE) the Catholic Church forbade marriage (and sexual intercourse) between Christians and Jews. The National Socialists followed this example in the so-called 'Nuremberg Laws' with which marriage and sexual intercourse outside marriage 'between Jews and members of the state who have German or kindred blood' was banned ('Law for the Protection of German Blood and German Honour' of 15 September 1935, 1, 2). So the Nazis shamelessly directed ideas which were similar to those developed by Jews under Ezra and Nehemiah and had been extended by a racist ideology against their Jewish fellow-citizens, heightened them in an antisemitic murderous craze and perpetrated a cruel massacre in this century.

In their legislation they even received support from a famous German New Testament scholar, Gerhard Kittel, who wrote in all seriousness: 'The radical eradication of connubium [marriage] between Jews and non-Jews carried out by National Socialism is not, as almost all the world outside Germany claims, an unprecedented act of cruelty against the Jews ... but in reality a healthy compulsion for Jews who assimilate to return to their own foundations and their laws' (Kittel 1943: 59). Here Kittel in his article, with a wealth of knowledge, demonstrated that the legislation under Ezra and Nehemiah was in no way the *foundation* of Judaism, but that 'assimilation' between Israel and the surrounding peoples was a feature of the earliest strata of the Old Testament and also continued in the period after Ezra and Nehemiah.

3

Anti-Judaism in the New Testament

A. A survey of the history of early Christianity and the relationships between the writings of the New Testament

Introduction

The New Testament consists of twenty-seven writings, of which only seven come from a person known to us through his own testimony (= Paul). The authors of all the other documents are anonymous in the truest sense. The superscriptions of the four Gospels come only from the second century, and the information about the senders of all the letters apart from those which are authentically Pauline is either false or gives the honorific title of a person whose life otherwise remains obscure. Thus 'the Elder' appears as author of II and III John and can only be identified by a bold combination with another old man of the early Christian period (cf. Lüdemann 1996: 171), or the Beloved Disciple who is said to have written the whole of the Gospel of John (cf. John 21.24).

The seven authentic writings are the following letters of the apostle Paul: Romans, I and II Corinthians, Galatians, Philippians, I Thessalonians and the letter to Philemon; the six other letters of Paul, namely Ephesians, Colossians, I and II Timothy, Titus and I Thessalonians make use of Paul's name as sender, and at the time of its canonization Hebrews was regarded as Pauline because its conclusion recalled letters of Paul (cf. Lüdemann 1995: 193–208).

The circumstances of the composition of the four Gospels are as follows. The earliest, the Gospel of Mark, was composed around 70 and was used by both Matthew and Luke independently of each other. In addition, Matthew and Luke used a lost collection of sayings of Jesus (= Q), of which the Gospel of Thomas, rediscovered at the end of 1945, is an offshoot. It also seems likely, but not certain, that John used the Gospel of Mark. The first three Gospels are called the synoptic Gospels (synopsis = looking together); from an investigation of how Matthew and/or Luke have taken up and worked over a text of Mark (= synoptic comparison) it can be discovered with great certainty how in using Mark they wanted to have the text before them understood. This methodological step of textual comparison will be important in the following chapter for discovering what the authors meant to say.

In the Acts of the Apostles Luke offers a kind of history of early Christianity. He writes it very schematically, beginning from Jerusalem (chs.1–5), as the history of Paul's mission (chs.16–28); at the centre (ch.15) as an axis stands the transition from the Jerusalem community to the Pauline mission among the Gentiles. Before this, the links between the Jerusalem community and the Pauline mission, the so-called Hellenists, are introduced (chs.6–12). And chs. 13–14 depict as a problem a model journey by the Hellenist Barnabas along with the future hero Paul.

Acts contains a wealth of individual material which needs to be given a precise chronological context on the basis of a framework first reconstructed from the letters of Paul (1989). Acts says nothing about the origin of many communities like those in Alexandria, Rome or Edessa. Moreover we learn nothing about where the Gospels were composed, although as Luke 1.1ff. shows, Luke was perhaps informed about this.

Chronologically speaking, the first community came into being in Jerusalem, and shortly after that communities developed in rapid succession in Damascus, Galilee, in the coastal cities of the Mediterranean and in Syrian Antioch – each with roots in Jerusalem. Mission in Greece was the work of Paul; the foundation of the community in Ephesus perhaps goes back to Apollos. After 70 Ephesus had been taken over by followers of the Presbyter John and became the home of the Johannine circle. Christianity probably entered Rome as early as the end of the 30s through the trade routes. In all probability Matthew belongs to Antioch, Mark possibly to Rome and Luke perhaps in the Aegean.

Paul's attempt to bind Gentile and Jewish Christians together proved impossible, at the latest after the loss of Jerusalem as the capital of Jewish Christianity. Mark is a Gentile Christian or presupposes a Gentile Christian community. Similarly Luke, Matthew and John, whether or not they are Jewish Christians, move rapidly away from the Jewish Christian foundation. So the line of development in early Christianity can be said to have led to a purely Gentile church as a result of the early proclamation and practice which exerted pressure towards the introduction of Gentiles, combined with the political event of the destruction of Jerusalem. Consequently, the Jewish Christians were forced to the periphery, and fifty years later they were regarded by the mainstream church as heretics.

Chronological framework

28	Appearance of John the Baptist
30	Execution of Jesus
33	Conversion of Paul
41	Expulsion of the Jews from Rome (Acts 18.2); I Thessalonians (or 50)
48	Jerusalem conference
50–53 (55)	The extant 'authentic' letters of Paul (possibly apart from I Thessalonians)
53 (56)	Journey of Paul to Jerusalem to bring the collection
64	Death of Paul in Rome
66	Beginning of the Jewish War
70	Siege of Jerusalem and destruction of the temple by the Romans; Gospel of Mark
70–90	Colossians, Ephesians, II Thessalonians, I Peter, Hebrews, James and Jude

90	Gospel of Matthew, Gospel of Luke, Acts
95	Revelation of John (or 110)
100–110	II/III John, Gospel of John, I John
130	I and II Timothy, Titus, II Peter

B. Anti-Judaism in the New Testament – a gesture of mercy?

What specifically is anti-Judaism?

I begin with a quotation from the fourth century in which almost all the anti-Jewish statements in the New Testament come to a head. To all appearances, here the seed sown by the New Testament authors shoots up. In the year 312 the Christian historian Eusebius writes the following about the unbelieving Jews:

> After the ascension of our Saviour (Acts 1.9) the Jews, in addition to their crime against him (viz. as being guilty of his death, I Thess. 2.15; Mark 15.6–15), had devised innumerable plots also against his apostles: first they put Stephen to death by stoning (Acts 7.58f.); and then, after him, James, who was the son of Zebedee and the brother of John, was beheaded (Acts 12.2f.) 2 and finally James, who was the first, after the ascension of our Saviour, to receive the throne of the episcopate there, departed this life in the manner we mentioned above. As for the other apostles, countless plots were laid against their lives, and they were banished from the land of Judaea; but they journeyed to all the nations to teach the message, in the power of the Christ who said to them, 'Go and make disciples of all the nations in my name'. (Matt. 28.19). Moreover, the people of the church at Jerusalem, in accordance with a certain oracle that was vouchsafed by way of revelation to approved men there, had been commanded to depart from the city before the war, and to inhabit a certain city of Peraea. They called it Pella. And when those who

believed in Christ had removed from Jerusalem, as if holy men had utterly deserted both the royal metropolis of the Jews itself and the whole land of Judaea, the justice of God then visited upon them all their acts of violence to Christ and his apostles, by destroying that generation of wicked persons root and branch from among men (*Church History* III, 5,2f.).

To summarize Eusebius's message: the unbelieving Jews have rightly been punished and exterminated because of their crime against Jesus.

Can the New Testament authors be made responsible for such harsh condemnations? Is this anti-Judaism, which is to be understood as a religiously motivated repudiation of the Jews, identical with the corresponding statements in the New Testament? At all events we have to take note of the different historical situations. Thus the New Testament authors doubtless found themselves in greater internal and external proximity to the Jews who did not believe in Christ, and who were certainly in the majority, and possibly they uttered anti-Jewish statements in polemical defence, with their backs to the wall. And in view of the fact that many Christians were themselves Jews, would we not do better to speak of polemic within Judaism instead of anti-Judaism? In that case Eusebius's generalizing attitude would need to be distinguished from the remarks of authors of individual New Testament writings who were conditioned by their situation.

However, different concepts by no means change the content of certain statements in the New Testament. For this reason we must guard against mitigating or explaining away the aggressively anti-Jewish content of some New Testament passages by a reference to a different situation and a different time. Finally, there should be no attempt formally to do away with the anti-Judaism of Christian origin by stilted theological observations. This happens where a distinction is made between numerous forms of anti-Judaism, and the reader no longer experiences or knows whether historically there was any religiously motivated repudiation of the Jews in early Christianity at all (this is the impression one gets on reading Klein 1982, who classifies anti-Judaism as defective perception, defective substance and defective language, but in fact diverts attention from the real issue). But enough of preliminary generalizations. The quotation from the fourth century given above shows specifically what anti-Judaism can consist of, and in what follows we shall be examine how far the anti-Judaism of New Testament authors corresponds to the anti-Judaism of Eusebius. If the answer is even approximately positive, the question then immediately arises: 'How can one confess the New Testament as a foundation document of faith, as the Word of God, if it contains a picture of the Jews, that people to which Jesus himself belonged, which is distorted by enmity and leads to hostility' (Stöhr 1967: 8).

I shall go through the writings of the New Testament in the order in which they are presumed to have been written.

I Thessalonians

The earliest extant letter of Paul from 41 or 50 contains very sharp polemic against the Jews (cf. the relevant commentaries and the works mentioned in Lüdemann 1996: 276 n.339; also Broer 1983: 59–91; Stegemann 1990: 54–64). I Thess. 2.14–16 states:

> 14 For you, brothers, became imitators of the churches of God in Christ Jesus which are in Judaea; for you suffered the same things from your own countrymen as they did from the Jews, 15 who killed both the Lord Jesus and the prophets, and drove us out and displease God and oppose all men 16 by hindering us from speaking to the Gentiles that they may be saved – so as always to fill up the measure of their sins. But God's wrath has come upon them at last.

Scholars have long recognized that at this point Paul is drawing on earlier models.

(a) For the statement that the Jews killed Jesus, reference should be made to the passion narratives in the Gospels, according to which the Jewish authorities hold a trial of Jesus, condemn him to death and hand him over to the Romans (see further 90–9 below), and the speeches in Acts, in which the Jews are called the murderers of Jesus (Acts 3.15; 4.10; 7.52).

(b) The accusation that the Jews killed the prophets corresponds to the Old Testament Jewish notion of the violent fate of the prophets, which is an interpretative theological statement (not a historical one). The Jews had already formulated it against themselves long beforehand.

> Neh. 9.26: 'Nevertheless they were disobedient and rebelled against you and cast your law behind their back and killed your prophets, who had warned them in order to turn them back to you, and they committed great blasphemies.'

> II Chron. 36.15–16: '15 The Lord, the God of their fathers, sent persistently to them by his messengers, because he had compassion on his people and on his dwelling place; 16 but they kept mocking the messengers of God, despising his words, and scoffing at his prophets, till the wrath of Yahweh rose against his people, till there was no remedy.'

(c) The accusation that the Jews are not pleasing to God and are enemies of all men also occurs in the polemic of pagan authors against the Jews. Thus for example at the end of the first century CE the Roman historian Tacitus writes that the Jews of his time have become increasingly more powerful and

> are extremely loyal to one another ... but toward every other people they feel only hate and enmity ... Those who are converted to their ways follow the same practices, and the earliest lesson they receive is to despise the gods, to disown their country and to regard their parents, children, and brothers as of no account ... (*Histories* V 5).

At around the same time Josephus writes:

> Apollonius Molo (a famous orator and grammarian of the second/first century BCE) describes the Jews as 'atheists and misanthropists' (*Against Apion* II, 148).

In the Greek translation of the Old Testament book of Esther the reason given for the command to murder all the Jews in the Persian empire is:

We understand that this people, and it alone, stands constantly in opposition to all men, perversely following a strange manner of life and laws, and is ill-disposed to our government, doing all the harm they can so that our kingdom may not attain stability (3.13e).

Paul's formulation is based closely on the traditions cited which may go back to a piece of tradition which has already been formed, and adds the comment: 'hindering us from speaking to the Gentiles that they may be saved' (I Thess. 2.16). This thesis is based on the observation that linguistically the clause mentioned displays Pauline features and that similar comments on traditions also appear elsewhere in Paul without the apostle drawing special attention to them. Thus the *aim* of the text in Paul is clear: the unbelieving Jews who are hindering Paul in his preaching to the Gentiles have finally fallen victim to the wrathful judgment of God.

However, the sense of the text written out by Paul, which on no account derives from a subsequent addition by an alien hand (cf. Lüdemann 1983: 25–7), does not alter the fact that the apostle has deliberately included the coarse polemic against the Jews in his letter, even if it was there before him in tradition. 'As Paul does not indicate any reservations about this text, we must assume that he adopts it because he shares its intentions' (Broer 1991:330). This insight arises from the widespread dissemination of the objection that the Jews are hostile to all people. Many who heard and read his letter knew this and immediately identified it 'as a typical pagan charge against the Jews' (Broer 1983: 81). In that case the adoption of this attack by Paul in particular may be polemic which deliberately brought out pagan resentment against his own people.

The positive counterpart to the negative verdict on unbelieving Judaism is Paul's view of the church made up of Jews and Gentiles. The Gentile Christians from Thessalonica have become imitators of the Jewish Christian community of Judaea. Their fellowship is one in suffering and in Christ. At the beginning of I Thessalonians Paul reminds his pagan community of their election (I Thess. 1.4), but this is equally true of the Jewish Christian churches in Judaea.

We can therefore say that with the call of the Gentiles, whose apostle Paul is, election has passed over to the church made up of Gentiles and Jews. For the unbelieving Jews who are hindering the mission to the Gentiles, all that is left is judgment.

Could Paul hold to this clear verdict? In this statement of repudiation is he thinking only of those Jews who are preventing him from preaching to the Gentiles and does he leave room, say, for the salvation of the remainder of Israel which, while unbelieving, does not hinder his preaching? Can the harsh saying in I Thess. 2 perhaps be explained by the exuberant, fiery character of I Thessalonians, in which the return of Jesus from heaven is feverishly longed for in the imminent future? What would Paul say if history continued and the Jews rejected the gospel not only as individuals, but as a majority? We should remember that I Thessalonians is Paul's earliest letter, in which such a development was not yet foreseeable.

I have discussed this question at length elsewhere (Lüdemann 1996: 95–102) and pointed out that towards the end of his life Paul arrives at a statement about Israel (= the Jews) which contradicts the harsh polemic in I Thessalonians. In Rom. 11.26 he writes that at the end of time all Israel will be saved. The reason for this is renewed reflection on God's saving action towards Israel in the light of the experience of the actual failure of the mission to the Jews. Here the statements in I Thess. 2.14ff. and Rom. 11.25f. which seem so contradictory may nevertheless derive from a relatively uniform starting-point once the way in which they are conditioned by their situation is taken into account: in I Thess. 2.14ff. the mission to the Gentiles is endangered, and Rom. 11.25f. reflects the possible loss of Jewish Christianity. Both letters are based on the indispensable presupposition that the church must consist of both Jews *and* Christians at the same time.

But the reality of early Christianity was not such that the vision of a church made up of Jews and Gentiles could win through. It derived from sheer wishful thinking. The historical reality underlying this sober verdict was as shocking as the *de facto* failure of the return of Jesus to materialize. Nevertheless here too Paul did not seem to be stumped. Evidently he suspected that very soon the Jewish-Christian part of the church would be lost and therefore warned the Gentile Christians in Rome not to lord it over the Jewish Christians. Indeed it even looks as if with his prophecy of the salvation of all Israel in Rom. 11 Paul wants to remedy his anti-Jewish slip-up in I Thess. 2 so that later Gentile Christians cannot appeal to him in their fight against the (unbelieving) Jews. Thus Paul leaves behind almost as a legacy an abiding reference to the rooting of the church in Israel, regardless of whether or not it is now totally Gentile Christian.

This legacy of Paul was *not* taken up in subsequent church history. Rather, I Thess. 2.16 was used as shorthand for the final judgment on Israel through the destruction of Jerusalem in 70 CE (cf. Kampling 1993) and Rom.11 was interpreted as conversion through mission to the Jews. A significantly sharper polemic against the Jews than that in I Thess. 2.14–16 was sparked off in other New Testament passages like Matt. 27.25 (see below, 92f.). All the Christian exegetes of I Thessalonians understood the alleged Jewish misanthropy as a hindrance to mission. But none read the charge in I Thessalonians which is so reminiscent of ancient antisemitism in the light of the remarks of Tacitus (see above, 83; cf. Kampling 1993).

The Gospel of Mark

The allegory of the wicked husbandmen (Mark 12.1–12)

1 And he began to speak to them in parables. 'A man planted a vineyard, and set a hedge around it, and dug a pit for the wine press, and built a tower, and let it out to tenants, and went into another country.

2 When the time came, he sent a servant to the tenants, to get from them some of the fruit of the vineyard.

3 And they took him and beat him, and sent him away empty-handed.

4 Again he sent to them another servant, and they wounded him in the head, and treated him shamefully.

5 And he sent another, and him they killed; and so with many others, some they beat and some they killed.

6 He had still one other, a beloved son; finally he sent him to them, saying, "They will respect my son."

7 But those tenants said to one another, "This is the heir; come, let us kill him, and the inheritance will be ours."

8 And they took him and killed him, and cast him out of the vineyard.

9 What will the owner of the vineyard do? He will come and destroy the tenants, and give the vineyard to others.

10 Have you not read this scripture: "The very stone which the builders rejected has become the head of the corner;

11 this was the Lord's doing, and it is marvellous in our eyes"?'

12 And they tried to arrest him, but feared the multitude, for they perceived that he had told the parable against them; so they left him and went away.

The text is an allegory which takes up the Song of the Vineyard in Isa. 5.1–7:

1 Let me sing for my beloved a love song concerning his vine-yard.

My beloved had a vineyard on a very fertile hill. 2 He digged it and cleared it of stones, and planted it with choice vines; he built a watchtower in the midst of it, and hewed out a wine vat in it; and he looked for it to yield grapes but it yielded wild grapes. 3 And now, O inhabitants of Jerusalem and men of Judah, judge, I pray you, between me and my vineyard. 4 What more was there to do for my vineyard, that I have not done in it? When I looked for it to yield grapes, why did it yield wild grapes? 5 And now I will tell you what I will do to my vineyard. I will remove its hedge, and it shall be devoured; I will break down its wall, and it shall be trampled down. 6 I will make it a waste; it shall not be pruned or hoed and briers and thorns shall grow up; I will also command the clouds that they rain no rain upon it. 7 For the vineyard of Yahweh of hosts is the house of Israel, and the men of Judah are his pleasant planting; and he looked for justice, but behold, bloodshed; for righteousness, but behold, a cry!

An allegory is to be found 'where a passage is first truly understood by transferring all its main terms (of course the conjunctions need not be included) to another sphere' (Jülicher 1963:59). This can be fully verified in Mark 12.1–12, the text of which certainly does not go back to Jesus. Here point by point each of the main terms stands for something else. The vineyard represents Israel, the husbandmen are its leaders, the owner is God, the servants are the prophets, the son is Christ, the punishment of the husbandmen stands for the rejection of Israel, 'the others' points towards the Gentile church.

The conclusion of the allegory is: *because the Jewish leaders have murdered Jesus, they themselves will be killed and Israel will be given to the Gentiles.* To endorse that by scriptural proof, in vv.10–11 a quotation from scripture (= Ps. 118.22f.) has been added. The image of the rejected stone which God has made the cornerstone is a popular text in the early church for the resurrection of Christ, who was *rejected* by the Jews.

Verse 12 emphasizes who are addressed in vv.1–11: the high priests, scribes and elders of Mark 11.27f., about whom Jesus had told this story. This tripartite group, and not the (Jewish) people, who are depicted in positive terms and who hindered immediate action against Jesus, represent the Jews in Mark's society who did not believe in Christ. As further justification for this view reference might be made to the corresponding accusation in I Thess. 2.15, which similarly talks of the killing of the prophets and the killing of Jesus by the Jews (see 81f. above), and above all to the account of the passion in Mark, in which the Jewish authorities lead the people astray into calling for the death of Jesus (for Mark 15.11–14 cf. below, 92).

How did the two other evangelists regard the story of the wicked husbandmen, which they read independently of each other in the Gospel of Mark?

The allegory of the wicked husbandmen in the Gospel of Matthew

Matthew 21.33–46 immediately shapes Mark's text into a sketch of salvation history from the making of the covenant on Sinai through the destruction of Jerusalem (21.41; cf.22.7) and the foundation of the Gentile church (21.43) to the last judgment (21.44). A particular emphasis in Matthew's interpretation becomes clear from two additions to the Markan text:

(a) Mark 12.9: in Matthew's version, 'The Lord of the vineyard ... will give the vineyard to others' becomes: 'The Lord of the vineyard... will let out the vineyard to other tenants who will give him the fruits in their seasons' (Matt. 21.41).

(b) Matthew adds the statement, 'Therefore I tell you, the kingdom of God will taken away from you and given to a nation producing the fruits of it' (Matt. 21.43), to the text of Mark. That means that God's kingdom will be taken away from Israel and given to a people which brings forth the 'fruits of the kingdom of God'. The word 'people' (Greek *ethnos*) refers to Gentiles and is also used in other passages in the Gospel of Matthew where these are certainly meant (cf. Matt. 10.5, 'Way of the Gentiles'; 28.19, 'Make disciples of all Gentiles!'). In other words, Matthew takes over all Mark's anti-Jewish statements; he gives them further point by emphasizing the explicit handing over of the vineyard to the Gentiles and denies Israel any promise. 'The church enters into its heritage as chosen people in so far as it keeps Jesus' commandments' (Luz 1993: 316).

The allegory of the wicked husbandmen in the Gospel of Luke

Luke 20.9–19 also intensifies the anti-Jewish interpretation and clarifies it christologically. Thus in accord with the passion narrative the son (as already in Matthew) is first cast out of the vineyard and then killed outside it (Luke 20.15; cf. Matt. 21.39). The christological reference is also made more precise in that in contrast to Mark 12.4f. the servants are not killed; the son is the first to be killed (Luke 20.15). Furthermore the second part of the scriptural quotation in Mark 12.10f. (Mark 12.11) is abbreviated and the following text is added: 'Every one who falls on that stone will be broken to pieces; but when it falls on any one it will crush him' (Luke 20.18). This threat is unambiguously aimed at the Jews. Cf. Acts 4.10f. (Peter addressing the authorities, elders and scribes in Jerusalem on the occasion of the healing of a sick man): '10 Be it known to you all, and to all the people of Israel, that by the name of Jesus Christ of Nazareth, whom you crucified, whom God raised from the dead, by him this man is standing before you well. 11 This is the stone which was rejected by you builders, but which has become the head of the corner.'

The conclusion to be drawn from the interpretation of the story of the wicked husbandmen by the synoptic evangelists is clearly that they are increasingly concerned to interpret the death of Jesus in anti-Jewish terms. To shape that effectively, an anti-Jewish interpretation was attributed to Jesus himself. No more effective condemnation could be uttered than that the Son of God had spoken about his own fate, had foisted all the blame for his death on the (unbelieving) Jews and of course predicted their punishment. Given this clear situation, how can it still be said that the Bible and especially the first three New Testament Gospels want to extend to all men and women the good news of God's mercy? In the view of Matthew, Luke and Mark, at least the unbelieving Jews were (and are) excluded from the grace of God.

The passion narrative (Mark 14–15)

The anti-Judaism of the Gospel of Mark is continued in the passion narrative. This cannot be understood without previously considering Jesus' three prophecies about his suffering (and his resurrection) which divide up the Gospel of Mark. They appear in 8.31; 9.31 and 10.32–34; either the author himself formulated the last two and found the first as tradition (cf. Strecker 1979), or he formed all three independently (cf. Reinbold 1994, 294 n.17). Their content is: *Jesus is going to Jerusalem to be put to death by the Jewish authorities.*

There is a parallel to this statement, made three times and put on the lips of Jesus himself, in Mark 3.6, a passage which has been formulated by the Second Evangelist: (after a healing on the sabbath) 'the Pharisees went out, and immediately held counsel with the Herodians against him, how to destroy him.' This plan runs right through the Gospel like a scarlet thread (cf. Mark 12.12: [the Jewish authorities] 'tried to arrest him, but feared the multitude, for they perceived that he had told the parable against them') and is then fulfilled in the passion narrative.

In view of this it is no longer surprising that in the Gospel of Mark all the high priests, elders and scribes condemn Jesus to death (Mark 14.64) and hand him over to Pilate (Mark 15.1). Pilate wants to let Jesus go, because he 'perceived that it was out of envy that the chief priests had delivered him up' (Mark 15.10). But his intention is then thwarted by the Jewish authorities. When Pilate wants to release Jesus, they incite the Jewish people to demand Jesus' crucifixion.

Mark 15.11–14: But the chief priests stirred up the crowd to have him release for them Barabbas instead. 12 And Pilate again said to them, 'Then what shall I do with the man whom you call the king of the Jews?' 13 And they cried out again, 'Crucify him!' 14 And Pilate said to them, 'Why, what evil has he done?' But they shouted all the more, 'Crucify him!'

If the differentiation throughout Mark between the Jewish elite and the Jewish people might suggest that only the elite were to blame for Jesus' death, the text passage just cited tells against such an assumption.

The conclusion must be that the anti-Judaism which becomes clear in Mark's interpretation of the parable of the vineyard has been intensified in the passion narrative: the Jews – i.e. high priests, scribes, elders, Pharisees and the people – bear sole responsibility for Jesus' death.

This tendency then continues brutally in the passion narratives of the Gospels of Matthew, Luke and John.

The passion narrative in the Gospel of Matthew

Matthew's aim can be discovered from a comparison of his account with that of Mark, which served him as a basis. There are hardly any deviations, but there are additions:

1. Judas, who had betrayed Jesus for thirty pieces of silver, repented of this, and brought them back to the high priests and elders, '4 saying, "I have sinned in betraying innocent blood." They said, "What is that to us? See to it yourself." 5 And throwing down the pieces of silver in the temple, he departed; and he went and hanged himself' (Matt. 27.4-5). Thus by way of anticipation the action against Jesus is presented as being reprehensible, and redactionally a devastating verdict is pronounced on the Jews who are hostile to Jesus. If a disciple who has betrayed Jesus can no longer compensate for his action despite his repentance and therefore must die, that is still nothing by comparison with the high priests and elders, who do not even repent of their action.

2. In Matthew Pilate's wife tells her husband, 'Have nothing to do with that righteous man, for I have suffered much over him today in a dream' (27.19). A Roman woman becomes witness to Jesus' innocence, whereas the Jewish people, spurred on by the authorities, calls for Jesus' death. The scene is sheer invention on Matthew's part and is therefore important for discovering his intention.

3. When Pilate recognizes that the Jewish people wants the crucifixion of Jesus, according to Matthew he takes water, washes his hands before the people (cf. Deut. 21.6; Ps. 26.6), and says, 'I am innocent of this man's blood; see to it yourselves' (Matt. 27.24). Accordingly Pilate endorses his wife's judgment: as a righteous man, Jesus is innocent. This heightens the guilt of the Jews further. The gesture, the performance by a pagan Roman 'of a Jewish biblical rite of expiation – washing the hands' (Luz 1993, 314), is very striking, and demonstrates Matthew's intention to foist blame for the death of Jesus on the Jewish people.

4. This intention is fully expressed in the way in which the Jewish people curses itself – a feature to be found only in Matthew, immediately after Pilate washes his hands: 'And all the people answered, "His blood be on us and on our children!"' (Matt. 27.25). With this verse Matthew is referring back to 23.34–36:

> 34 Therefore I send you prophets and wise men and scribes, some of whom you will kill and crucify, and some you will scourge in your synagogues and persecute from town to town, 35 that upon you may come all the righteous blood shed on earth, from the blood of innocent Abel to the blood of Zechariah the son of Barachiah, whom you murdered between the sanctuary and the altar. 36 Truly, I say to you, all this will come upon this generation.

In v. 25, in contrast to v. 24, where the Greek word *ochlos* is used, Matthew uses a term for 'the people' (*laos*) which in the Greek Bible generally denotes the special religious position of Israel. 'All Israel as the people chosen by Yahweh takes the blame for his death on its shoulders and those of all generations ... The Jews could act in this way only because guilt over the death of Jesus was not a question for them' (Broer 1989: 109). Granted, Pilate gave the order for the crucifixion, but according to Matthew Israel bears the blame for Jesus' death, and because of this it has finally forfeited its election. Even the Jews must assent to this because, convinced of Jesus' guilt, they uttered a conditional curse on themselves. But as Jesus' innocence is clear, they are responsible for the consequences, so that Jesus' blood comes upon them and their children. None of the anti-Jewish statements in the New Testament has provoked so much murder, misery and despair among Jews in subsequent church history as this (for the history of the exegesis of Matt. 27.25 cf. Kampling 1984).

The passion narrative in the Gospel of Luke

In the account of the trial before Pilate (Luke 23.2–5), Luke follows his basis in Mark, but with significant changes: v.2 ('... And they began to accuse him, saying, "We found this man perverting our nation, and forbidding us to give tribute to Caesar, and saying that he himself is Christ a king"') has been added to Mark's text and refers back to Luke 20.20–26 ('Paying tax to Caesar'):

> 20 So they (= the scribes and high priests) watched him, and sent spies, who pretended to be sincere, that they might take hold of what he said, so as to deliver him up to the authority and jurisdiction of the governor. 21 They asked him, 'Teacher, we know that you speak and teach rightly, and show no partiality but truly teach the way of God. 22 Is it lawful for us to give tribute to Caesar, or not?' 23 But he perceived their craftiness, and said to them, 24 'Show me a coin. Whose likeness and inscription has it?' They said, 'Caesar's.' 25 He said to them, 'Then render to Caesar the things that are Caesar's, and to God the things that are God's.' 26 And they were not able in the presence of the people to catch him by what he said; but marvelling at his answer they were silent.

By bringing out the connection between Luke 23.2 and 20.20–26, Luke makes it clear that the accusation of the Jewish authorities is based on a lie. For Jesus had explicitly endorsed the payment of taxes. The Jewish action against Jesus is therefore grounded in a malicious calumniation, but Pilate did not fall for it. This is clear from his two statements which Luke has similarly added to his Markan basis:

> Luke 23.4: 'And Pilate said to the chief priests and the multitudes, "I find no crime in this man."'
>
> Luke 23.13–16: 'Pilate then called together the chief priests and the rulers and the people, 14 and said to them, "You brought me this man as one who was perverting the people; and after examining him before you, behold, I did not find this man guilty of any of your charges against him; 15 neither did Herod, for he sent him back to us. Behold, nothing deserving death has been done by him; 16 I will therefore chastize him and release him."'

At the same time, it is clear from these two texts added to the Markan basis that like his predecessors, Luke sees the Jewish elite *and* the people as a unity. Therefore the designation 'the Jews' is also hostile when it is related to this assignation of guilt.

This reaches a climax in Luke's assertion that Jews – not Romans – executed Jesus. Luke depicts the scourging scene (Mark 15.16–20) in such a way that Jesus is taken away immediately after he has been handed over. Accordingly the text has to be read as follows: Pilate handed over Jesus to the will of the Jews (23.25). They led him away (26) .... They crucified him (33). It follows from this that those who call for Jesus' death also execute him. Luke 24.20 confirms that the Third Evangelist really thought this. Here the disciples on the Emmaus road explain to the risen Jesus, who meets them unrecognized in the form of a traveller, that the high priests and authorities handed Jesus over to suffer the death penalty and crucified him (for the redactional character of his verse cf. Lüdemann 1994: 141). Here the fact that the people are not mentioned can hardly lead to the assumption that according to Luke responsibility for the death of Jesus is to be restricted to the Jewish elite. For in addition to the attribution of guilt to the people in Luke 23.4, 13–16, which has been cited, this group is also explicitly 'incriminated' in Acts 3.15 (cf. v.12).

The conclusion to be drawn from Luke's account of the passion is that the anti-Judaism is further heightened by comparison with Mark, as is the innocence of the Roman Pilate. In both respects Matthew and Luke independently agree with each other.

The passion narrative in the Gospel of John

The hearing before the Sanhedrin related by all three Synoptic Gospels no longer appears in John. The Fourth Evangelist reports only a hearing before Pilate (John 18.28–19.16).

Previously Jesus has been interrogated by the high priest Annas (John 18.19–23), who hands him over fettered to the high priest Caiaphas (John 18.24). From there Jesus goes to Pilate. The latter must be concerned with the affair because the Jews bring the prisoner Jesus to him. On the one hand they appear as accusers before Pilate the judge, and on the other they ask the governor to carry out a valid legal verdict which they have passed, but which they have not pronounced explicitly. Accordingly the Jews are depicted in a perplexing way. Julius Wellhausen aptly observes: 'The hearing before Annas is meant to be a hearing and is not; that before Pilate is not meant to be one and is, though only materially and not formally' (Wellhausen 1908: 83). He continues: Pilate 'is involved, not in any public proceedings with Jesus, but in a private interview within the praetorium. The Jews remain outside and learn something about the state of his dealings with the accused only through him. For this purpose he constantly has to run to and fro between the parties, in and out of the praetorium' (Wellhausen 1908: 83f.). This is no 'muddle', as Wellhausen (ibid.) thinks, but a literary artifice by which the narrator creates two different scenes and has the drama played out on two stages (cf. Haenchen 1967: 64). But it also happens in order to involve the Jews in the process from the beginning. For that reason John does not have a real hearing before the Sanhedrin. But he inserts the Jews into the account of the Roman trial and thus intensifies their guilt.

Although there is no real hearing before the Sanhedrin, the Jews are directly involved in the trial of Jesus. Moreover, they are incriminated even more because they have handed over Jesus (John 18.35), and Jesus explicitly presents this as wickedness: 'He who has delivered me to you (viz. Pilate) has the greater sin.'

Exoneration of Pilate goes hand in hand with the heightened attribution of guilt to the Jews. Pilate expresses his conviction of Jesus' innocence several times (18.38; 19.4,6) and repeatedly attempts to set the prisoner free (18.39; 19.1–5, 12).

The apologetic towards the Roman state at the expense of the Jews which is at work in John is further intensified in the Gospel of Peter, which comes from the beginning of the second century. Here Pilate is a friend of Joseph of Arimathea (2.3) and thus indirectly a friend of Jesus. At the beginning of the third century the church fathers Tertullian and Origen finally depict the Roman governor as a Christian (cf. Bauer 1972: 184–92 [with further information on the role of Pilate in early Christian literature]).

Who really condemned Jesus to death?

Jesus' crucifixion, a Roman form of execution, is an assured fact. Three conclusions can be drawn from this mode of death:

(a) Romans put Jesus to death;
(b) there were Roman legal proceedings beforehand;
(c) Jesus was condemned for a political crime.

Further historical details can be extracted only on the basis of source criticism. Literary-critical analysis leads to the verdict that both Matthew and Luke and probably also John are *dependent* on Mark's report. That means that only the Marcan narrative can be used in establishing facts.

Mark's account of the trial and condemnation of Jesus before the Sanhedrin (Mark 14.53–65) is in any case secondary and has been composed either by Mark himself (cf. Winter 1962) or by a predecessor. At all events it corresponds item by item to the hearing before Pilate (Mark 15.1–5, 15b/20a). Compare the parallels:

Jesus before the Sanhedrin	Jesus before Pilate
14.53a	15.1
14.55	15.3
14.60	15.4
14.61a	15.5
14.61b	15.2
14.62	15.2
14.64	15.15
14.65	15.16–20

It follows from this that the hearing before the Sanhedrin has been composed on the basis of a tradition of the hearing before Pilate and therefore is not to be considered as a historical report. The apologetic features (cf. 15.10) and indications of hostility to the Jews (cf. 15.11–14) contained in the accounts of the hearing before Pilate which have been pointed out above (90) are certainly to be deleted.

Historically, what then remain are the following historical data:

(a) a trial before the Roman prefect Pilate;
(b) a political calumniation on the part of the Jerusalem priesthood – which alone led Pilate to intervene;
(c) the crucifixion of Jesus.

Pilate – a mild and perceptive ruler?

The New Testament Gospels depict Pilate as a perceptive man who sees through the Jewish authorities and recognizes Jesus' innocence. What is the historical probability of such a verdict? The available sources relating to Pilate show quite a different picture from that sketched in the New Testament. Here are two (and more could easily be added):

(a) The Jewish philosopher Philo, a contemporary of the apostle Paul, reports that under Pilate there were 'corruption, acts of violence, robberies, maltreatments, insults, continual executions without trial, endless and intolerable cruelties' (Philo, *Leg.*38).

(b) Josephus relates that Pilate misused the temple treasure in Jerusalem to build an aqueduct into the city. He writes:

> The crowd was very indignant about this, and when Pilate came to Jerusalem, they thronged before his tribunal and made a clamour about it. Now since he had been apprised beforehand of this disturbance, Pilate mixed his own soldiers, wearing their armour, in among the crowd, but ordered them to conceal themselves in ordinary dress, and not to use their swords, but to beat with clubs those who cried out. He then gave the signal from his tribunal: the Jews were so badly beaten that many of them perished from the blows they received and many others were trodden to death as their fellow-countrymen fled. Terrified by the fate of those who had been killed, the people fell silent (*Jewish War* II, 175–177).

It is in keeping with the picture of a cruel Roman official that Luke 13.1 presupposes that Pilate had a number of Galileans killed when they were presenting their offerings in the Jerusalem temple.

Our conclusion must be that the implication of the New Testament Gospels that Pilate was a perceptive ruler is a great deception. Their view that Pilate had merely been a tool of the Jews so that these could really carry out their death sentence is sheer wishful thinking and historically inaccurate (for the historical Pilate see Schürer 1973: 383–7; Lémonon 1981).

The claim that the Jews were guilty of the death of Jesus

The learned church father Origen (185/6–254) wrote on Matt. 27.25 and the consequences which it had for the Jews: 'Therefore they not only became guilty of the blood of the prophets, but also filled up the measure of their fathers and became guilty of the blood of Christ ... Therefore the blood of Jesus came not only upon those who lived formerly but also upon all subsequent generations of Jews to the consummation' (Vogt 1993: 324).

These words contain the average Christian view of the Jews as this has developed in an intellectual tradition extending over centuries, and as it has been predominant from earliest Christianity to modern times. Today historians have explained that the way in which the Jews are incriminated by the New Testament Gospels is historically untrue. As is generally recognized by scholars, this results from their apologetic tendency which, according Paul's Winter's apt judgment, seeks to exonerate the Romans and present the Jews as enemies.

The same New Testament scholars who are unanimous in this verdict often say 'that historical facts are unimportant ... History is unimportant and dead, and all that matters is the interpretation which elevates itself above the facts of what once happened' (Winter 1967: 104). Paul Winter continues: 'What is left by the wayside in this approach is the truth: the unadorned, unkerygmatized, unprofound truth of the facts. What gets short shrift in this approach is the conscience' (ibid.). With reference to the claim that the Jews were historically guilty of the death of Jesus, a claim which can still be heard and is not sufficiently contradicted, he concludes: 'Or will Christianity, rich in cultural goods and values, continue to the end of time – and allow itself the luxury of a theology for which others pay the bill?' (ibid.).

A further question immediately arises: in view of this brutal historical evidence and in view of the historical falsification of the facts, how can one associate the New Testament Gospels with the word of God which allegedly offers all men and women the good news of God's mercy? *Does not a deep shadow fall from this, its dark side, on everything else that they wrote, with devastating consequences for the Jews in subsequent church history?* Can we still rely on the evangelists if they so twisted historical truth at a decisive point?

The Gospel of Matthew

I shall now go on to discuss three passages which give further insight into Matthew's anti-Judaism: the parable of the wedding feast (22.1–14), the discourse against scribes and Pharisees (23.1–38) and the resurrection stories (27.62–28.20).

The parable of the wedding feast (Matt. 22.1–14)

The parable of the wedding feast follows that of the wicked husbandmen (21.33–46), the purpose of which was already defined on 89 above. It runs: the church replaces Israel in so far as it keeps Jesus' words. Israel is totally disqualified and has been completely robbed of its salvation by the destruction of Jerusalem.

A similar intention can be established for the parable of the wedding feast. To make them more quickly identifiable, the anti-Jewish passages and their positive counterparts, aimed at the Gentiles, have been printed in italics.

22.1 Again Jesus spoke to them in parables, saying, 2 'The kingdom of heaven may be compared to a king who gave a marriage feast for his son, 3 and sent his servants to call those who were invited to the marriage feast; but they would not come. 4 Again he sent other servants, saying, 'Tell those who are invited, Behold, I have made ready my dinner, my oxen and my fat calves are killed, and everything is ready; come to the marriage feast.' 5 But they made light of it and went off, one to his farm, another to his business, 6 while the rest seized his servants, treated them shamefully, and killed them. *7 The king was angry, and he sent his troops and destroyed those murderers and burned their city.* 8 Then he said to his servants, 'The wedding is ready, but those invited were not worthy. *9 Go therefore to the thoroughfares*, and invite to the marriage feast as many as you find.' 10 And those servants *went out into the streets* and gathered all whom they found, both bad and good; so the wedding hall was filled with guests. 11 But when the king came in to look at the guests, he saw there a man who had no wedding garment; 12 and he said to him, 'Friend, how did you get in here without a wedding garment?' And he was speechless. 13 Then the king said to the attendants, 'Bind him hand and foot, and cast him into the outer darkness; there men will weep and gnash their teeth.' 14 For many are called, but few are chosen.

Verse 1 is Matthew's introduction. Verses 2–20, like Luke 14.16–24 (see 108f. below), go back to Q. Matthew has interpreted the Q tradition which he had before him by making additions. Verses 11–14 were originally an independent parable. It was first added here by Matthew or already belonged to the Q tradition which he has used.

Verses 2–10 are an allegory of salvation, but this time about the period after Easter. The king, i.e. God, arranges a feast for his son, namely Jesus Christ. Therefore he cannot bring the invitation (as in Luke = Q). Matthew 'transforms the servant, who is in the singular in Luke, into a plurality of servants, which can only be understood to denote the apostles. By their preaching of the gospel they invite the Jews to enter the kingdom of God, but come up against contemptuous indifference among the upper classes' (Wellhausen 1914: 105f.). The first group of servants (v.3) stands for the prophets and the repudiation of their message; the second group (v.4) denotes the apostles and missionaries sent to Israel (Jerusalem) and the maltreatment and martyrdom (v.6) suffered by some of them. The sending on to the streets (vv.9f.) suggests the Gentile mission; the entry into the wedding feast (v.10b) suggests a baptism (cf. Jeremias 1972: 69). The vivid statement in v.7 shows an intensification of anti-Judaism: the murderous Jews are killed and their city (= Jerusalem) is set on fire. Matthew is looking back on the Jewish War in 70 CE.

Like the allegory of the wicked husbandmen, vv.11–14 inculcate the role of good works and are a further indication that conduct is important for Matthew. For v.9, which tells of an indiscriminate invitation of guests, could have given the impression of ethical indifference.

The discourse against scribes and Pharisees

Here Matthew has made a large insertion, using Q (Luke 11.37–52; 13.34f.). In Mark this passage is addressed to the people (12.37f.) and in Matthew also to the disciples (Matt. 23.1, 8–12). Mark only speaks of scribes (Mark 12.38), whereas Matthew brings together scribes and Pharisees (Matt. 23.2), and Luke makes an artificial distinction between them (Luke 11.39,46). Matthew leaves the discourses in the situation of Mark 12.38–40; here the scribe in Mark who was not far from the kingdom of God (Mark 12.34) has become a mere tempter (Matt. 22.35) – a gloomy pointer to the way in which, in the view of the first evangelist, Jesus will pour fire and brimstone upon the scribes and Pharisees.

In composing discourses Matthew proves to be an author of great distinction. This is true not only of his most famous composition, the Sermon on the Mount (Matt. 5–7), but also of the present discourse against scribes and Pharisees in ch.23:

> 1. Then said Jesus to the crowds and to his disciples, 2 'The scribes and the Pharisees sit on Moses' seat; 3 so practise and observe whatever they tell you, but not what they do; for they preach, but do not practise. 4 They bind heavy burdens, hard to bear, and lay them on men's shoulders; but they themselves will not move them with their finger. 5 They do all their deeds to be seen by men; for they make their phylacteries broad and their fringes long 6 and they love the place of honour at feasts and the best seats in the synagogues, 7 and salutations in the market places, and being called rabbi by men. 8 But you are not to be called rabbi, for you have one teacher, and you are all brethren. 9 And call no man your father on earth, for you have one Father, who is in heaven. 10 Neither be called masters, for you have one master, the Christ. 11 He who is greatest among you shall be your servant; 12 whoever exalts himself will be humbled, and whoever humbles himself will be exalted.
>
>   13 *Woe to you, scribes and Pharisees, hypocrites!* because you shut the kingdom of heaven against men; for you

neither enter yourselves, nor allow those who would enter to go in.

15 *Woe to you, scribes and Pharisees, hypocrites*! for you traverse sea and land to make a single proselyte, and when he becomes a proselyte, you make him twice as much a child of hell as yourselves.

16 Woe to you, blind guides, who say, "If any one swears by the temple, it is nothing; but if any one swears by the gold of the temple, he is bound by his oath." 17 You blind fools! For which is greater, the gold or the temple that has made the gold sacred? 18 And you say, "If any one swears by the altar, it is nothing; but if any one swears by the gift that is on the altar, he is bound by his oath." 19 You blind men! For which is greater, the gift or the altar that makes the gift sacred? 20 So he who swears by the altar, swears by it and by everything on it; 21 and he who swears by the temple, swears by it and by him who dwells in it; 22 and he who swears by heaven, swears by the throne of God and by him who sits upon it.

23 *Woe to you, scribes and Pharisees, hypocrites*! for you tithe mint and dill and cumin, and have neglected the weightier matters of the law, justice and mercy and faith; these you ought to have done, without neglecting the others. 24 You blind guides, straining out a gnat and swallowing a camel!

25 *Woe to you, scribes and Pharisees, hypocrites*! for you cleanse the outside of the cup and of the plate, but inside they are full of extortion and rapacity. 26 You blind Pharisee! first cleanse the inside of the cup and of the plate, that the outside also may be clean.

27 *Woe to you, scribes and Pharisees, hypocrites*! for you are like whitewashed tombs, which outwardly appear beautiful, but within they are full of dead men's bones and all uncleanness. 28 So you also outwardly appear righteous to men, but within you are full of hypocrisy and iniquity.

29 *Woe to you, scribes and Pharisees, hypocrites*! for you build the tombs of the prophets and adorn the monuments of the righteous, 30 saying, "If we had lived in the days of our

fathers, we would not have taken part with them in shedding the blood of the prophets." 31 Thus you witness against your-selves, that you are sons of those who murdered the prophets. 32 Fill up, then, the measure of your fathers. 33 You serpents, you brood of vipers, how are you to escape being sentenced to hell? 34 Therefore I send you prophets and wise men and scribes, some of whom you will kill and crucify, and some you will scourge in your synagogues and persecute from town to town, 35 that upon you may come all the righteous blood shed on earth, from the blood of innocent Abel to the blood of Zechariah the son of Barachiah, whom you murdered between the sanctuary and the altar. 36 Truly, I say to you, all this will come upon this generation.

37 O Jerusalem, Jerusalem, killing the prophets and stoning those who are sent to you! How often would I have gathered your children together as a hen gathers her brood under her wings, and you would not! 38 Behold, your house is forsaken and desolate (Jer. 22.5; Ps. 69.26).'

The discourse begins with words acknowledging the Jewish leaders (vv.1–2a). Then the tone changes: they do not do what they teach and seek only outward recognition (vv.2b–7). They are not suitable as a model because of this contradiction within themselves. This anticipates the main charge of *hypocrisy* which follows later. Granted, the 'short section on Christian humility (vv.8–12) ... once again offers some rest after the charges of vv.3–7' (Haenchen 1965: 49). But then the storm bursts. Seven woes brand the scribes and Pharisees as hypocrites (vv.13–33). The number seven is deliberately used by Matthew to increase the weight of the charge. He may have composed the third woe himself for this purpose – evident from the somewhat different introduction (v.16) – whereas the others, whose harsh polemic can be explained by the fact that these are controversies within an association of synagogues (cf. Becker 1990; Newport 1995 [lit.]), go back to tradition.

Whereas the preaching of judgment up to v.33 was only about the scribes and Pharisees, in vv.34–36 this is no longer the case. Here the formal address to the Pharisees and scribes is dropped. The Christian prophets, wise men and scribes (sic!) indicate Matthew's time. They will suffer the fate of being killed, crucified and scourged (cf. Matt. 10.17; 22.6), and by the very Pharisees and scribes whom Jesus chastizes for their hypocrisy. Verses 35f. show that Matthew is thinking of a judgment on all Israel. 'This is the goal of the chapter' (Luz 1993: 313f.; cf. also Becker 1990: 235). The lament over Jerusalem (vv.37f.) presupposes a punishment consisting in the devastation of Jerusalem (in the Jewish War). 'The city is not just devastated, but it is devastated and is to *continue to lie* in ruins' (Wellhausen 1914: 115).

The sharpness and polemic of these condemnations by Matthew are made even more questionable by the fact that they are not simply stated as the words of a prophet but are attributed to Jesus himself.

The resurrection stories (Matt. 27.62–28.20)

The resurrection stories in the Gospel of Matthew have no anti-Jewish features where they presuppose the Gospel of Mark (cf. Matt. 28.1, 5–10 = Mark 16.1–8). However, in the special material things are different.

First, the Gospel of Mark contains a story of guards at the tomb (Matt. 27.62–66; 28.11–15), which forms the framework for the story of the visit of the women to the empty tomb told in connection with Mark 16.1–8. Here Matt. 28.13 refers to 27.64. Though they know it to be untrue, the soldiers are to spread the rumour that the disciples stole the body of Jesus while they themselves were sleeping. Previously the Jewish authorities had already feared such a robbery of the tomb (Matt. 27.64). Now, since Jesus is really risen, they bribe the soldiers to spread this false information. so they are impudent liars. We can see here how the criticism is intensified just as it is in Matt. 23.1–36 in relation to Mark 12.37b–40, which is used as a basis and expanded.

Secondly, at the end of the Gospel of Matthew there is a further Easter story (28.16–20). It is anti-Jewish in that according to it the Christian message is no longer to be extended to Israel, whereas according to Matt. 10.5f. the disciples had still been sent exclusively to the lost sheep of the house of Israel and not to the Gentiles: '5 ... Go nowhere among the nations, and enter no town of the Samaritans, 6 but go rather to the lost sheep of the house of Israel.' The group targeted by the mission command (28.19: 'Go and make disciples of all nations ...'), which deliberately refers back to Matt. 10.5f., consists exclusively of Gentiles. This is suggested first by the consideration that because of the reference back from Matt. 28.19 to Matt. 10.5f., in both passages 'nations' (*ethne*) needs to have the same meaning. Now because of the contrast with Israel, in Matt. 10.5 the nations are clearly understood as Gentiles. Secondly, Matthew could have hardly classed the Jews under the heading of nations; he still lived and thought too much in a Jewish framework, in which the term 'nations' exclusively denoted Gentiles (and not Jews). The dialogue with Israel has finally been broken off. The mission of the disciples to Israel is not confirmed in the mission charge, but is expressly done away with and transcended.

From an ecclesiological perspective the mission to all Gentiles presupposes a substitution theory. The church of the Gentiles takes the place of Israel. Unbelieving Israel is condemned to hell in view of the guilt which it has taken upon itself by killing Jesus and his emissaries. (There is a different view of the role of unbelieving Israel in Matthew's time in Levine 1988: 193–278 [with bibliography], according to whom the Jews continue to remain the focal point for Christian preaching.)

Luke-Acts

The salvation-historical perspective

In view of the positive description of Jewish customs in the Gospel of Luke and Acts, an analysis of the anti-Judaism in Luke-Acts may at first sight seem surprising. For the persons depicted there observe the Jewish customs. Jesus is circumcised on the eighth day (Luke 2.21) and at the age of twelve is already remaining in the temple (Luke 2.46), following the same practice as will later be observed by the first community (Luke 24.53; Acts 2.46; 3.1; 5.42). Paul also observes the law strictly: he visits the synagogue every sabbath, circumcises his companion Timothy (Acts 16.3), takes part in the Jewish ritual of the Nazirate (Acts 21.23–26), and as a Christian is proud of having been a Pharisee (Acts 26.5).

But this kind of description seems to go back to the claim made by Luke in his prologue (Luke 1.1–4) that he is giving a historical account. In that case it would be part of his historicizing tendency, which does not give any direct indication of his theological view. Here

> the relationship between church and Judaism is governed by a gradual separation. Luke does not teach an abrupt break in the election of Israel in salvation history of the kind that can be established in Matthew and also in Mark. Rather, after the death and resurrection of Jesus the church remains allied to Judaism. Its preaching is addressed to the Jews. That is shown by the story of Pentecost (Acts 2.1–13), in which the catalogue of peoples (2.9–11) relates not to Gentiles but to Diaspora Jews who live in various countries outside Palestine (Strecker 1995: 433f.).

It is the 'repudiation of Christian preaching by the Jews which creates an independent church, consisting of Jews and Gentiles, a church which knows that it is bound up with the Jewish people of God in a continuous salvation history and which thus understands itself as the guardian of the authentic legacy of Judaism' (Strecker 1995: 434). The theological assessment of this should not be that Luke sees the church as an extension of Israel *(pace* Marguerat 1994: 250, referring to Acts 13.47 – but Old Testament quotations are always a doubtful criterion for defining a redactional significance in context), though it is certain that historically, Lukan Christianity represents an ongoing development of a Greek-speaking Judaism.

A distinction is to be made between this perspective, grounded in salvation history, and the thrust of statements focussed directly on the present. The anti-Jewish content of the Lukan version of the allegory of the wicked husbandmen (Luke 20.9–19) was already evident, and it was clear from the passion narrative, in which Luke goes beyond Mark in both foisting the blame for the execution of Jesus on the Jews and further exonerating the Roman Pilate (cf. also Acts 3.15; 4.10; 7.52; 13.17–29 for the responsibility of the Jewish authorities and the Jewish people for the death of Jesus).

Only textual analyses can shed further light on the anti-Judaism of Luke-Acts.

The parable of the banquet (Luke 14.15–24)

15 When one of those who sat at table with him heard this, he said to him, 'Blessed is he who shall eat bread in the kingdom of God!' 16 But he said to him, 'A man once gave a great banquet, and invited many; 17 and at the time for the banquet he sent his servant to say to those who had been invited, "Come; for all is now ready." 18 But they all alike began to make excuses. The first said to him, "I have bought a field, and I must go out and see it; I pray you, have me excused." 19 And another said, "I have bought five yoke of oxen, and I go to examine them; I pray you, have me excused." 20 And another said, "I have married a wife, and therefore I cannot come." 21 So the servant came and reported this to his master. Then the householder in anger said to his servant, "Go out quickly to the streets and lanes of the city, and bring in the poor and maimed and blind and lame." 22 And the servant said, "Sir, what you commanded has been done, and still there is room." 23 And the master said to the servant, "Go out to the highways and hedges, and compel people to come in, that my house may be filled. 24 For I tell you, none of those men who were invited shall taste my banquet."'

As the Matthaean parallel (22.10) shows, the parable of the

banquet comes from the Q tradition. Three points need to be brought out in the Lukan interpretation of the parable: (a) in the content of the Gospel of Luke the parable serves as a prime example of the demand made in Luke 14.12–14 to invite the poorest, since the same list appears in v.21 as appears in v.13 ('poor, maimed, lame, blind').

(b) A second point of the parable for Luke becomes clear in v.23: the people living outside the city might refer to the Gentiles (cf. Jeremias 1972: 64).

(c) The third point lies in v.24, which explicitly denies those originally invited (namely the Jews) access to the meal because they did not accept the invitation. What is only stated by Luke is reinforced by Matthew, who elaborates it in violent terms: the (unbelieving) Jews are murdered and excluded from salvation for ever (see above 100f.).

The report of Paul's activity in Rome (Acts 28.17–31)

Luke's anti-Judaism is evident in Acts, where he reports in stereotypical fashion that while Paul proclaims the gospel to the Jews, the Jews regularly reject this message, with the result that Paul becomes purely a missionary to the Gentiles. This anti-Jewish pattern reaches a climax at the end of Acts. If we assume that the leading perspective of the author will become clear especially at the conclusion of a literary work, an investigation of the end of Acts promises to shed further light on Luke's anti-Judaism.

17 After three days Paul called together the local leaders of the Jews; and when they had gathered, he said to them, 'Brethren, though I had done nothing against the people or the customs of our fathers, yet I was delivered prisoner from Jerusalem into the hands of the Romans. 18 When they had examined me, they wished to set me at liberty, because there was no reason for the death penalty in my case. 19 But when the Jews objected, I was compelled to appeal to Caesar – though I had no charge to bring against my nation. 20 For this reason therefore I have asked to see you and speak with

you, since it is because of the hope of Israel that I am bound with this chain.'

21 And they said to him, 'We have received no letters from Judaea about you, and none of the brethren coming here has reported or spoken any evil about you. 22 But we desire to hear from you what your views are; for with regard to this sect we know that everywhere it is spoken against.' 23 When they had appointed a day for him, they came to him at his lodging in great numbers. And he expounded the matter to them from morning till evening, testifying to the kingdom of God and trying to convince them about Jesus both from the law of Moses and from the prophets. 24 And some were convinced by what he said, while others disbelieved. 25 So, as they disagreed among themselves, they departed, after Paul had made one statement: 'The Holy Spirit was right in saying to your fathers through Isaiah the prophet: 26 "Go to this people, and say, You shall indeed hear but never understand, and you shall indeed see but never perceive. 27 For this people's heart has grown dull, and their ears are heavy of hearing, and their eyes they have closed; lest they should perceive with their eyes, and hear with their ears, and understand with their heart, and turn for me to heal them." 28 *Let it be known to you then that this salvation of God has been sent to the Gentiles; they will hear it.*'

30 And he lived there two whole years at his own expense, and welcomed all who came to him, 31 preaching the kingdom of God and teaching about the Lord Jesus Christ quite openly and unhindered.

Paul presents himself to the Jews of Rome as a Jewish patriot: he is bound with chains 'for the hope of Israel' (v.20). The sympathy of the Jews is expressed in their thirst for knowledge and further by the statement that they have heard nothing negative about Paul.

However, the whole text is only friendly to the unbelieving Jews on the surface. Granted, people have used v.24 as a sign of openness to the relationship between Christians and Jews in

Luke's time (cf. Marguerat 1994: 261). But in v.24 (as in Acts 17.4; 19.9) the emphasis lies on the fact that Paul's preaching causes a split among the Jews. Moreover the only possible conclusion which can still be drawn from Paul's controversy with the Jews is that Luke is using a quotation from the prophecy of Isaiah to explain that the eyes of the Jews remain closed, indeed that their eyes are closed in order that (!) they do not understand or are converted. We must imagine that in Luke's time the mission to the Jews had come to grief and that the author of Acts has to explain why now God's salvation is exclusively granted to the Gentiles, whereas the Jews persist – indeed must persist – in unbelief (among others, Weatherly 1994: 150, 155, differs, cf. 275: 'The mission to Jews does not appear to be over, and the church remains composed of both Jews and Gentiles').

Note at the end the statement that in Rome Paul preaches the gospel unhindered. This is an apologetic ploy directed towards Roman readers, who are meant to be won over to Luke's version of Christianity by it.

Summing up the Lukan part, it can be said that Luke has written a salvation history which is governed by a gradual detachment of the church from Israel until at the end of Acts the final separation of the two is demonstrated and the honorific title 'Israel' is claimed for Luke's church. (All three synoptic Gospels, and the Gospel of John, which we shall go on to consider, are agreed on the last point.) Luke often inserts thrusts against the Jews into the historicizing text of the Gospel and Acts and thus gives information about his real standpoint (compare with the above description Sanders 1987).

The Gospel of John

The Gospel of John is the latest of the four New Testament Gospels. The first results about the anti-Judaism it contains were produced by a comparison of his account of the passion with the accounts in the Synoptic Gospels. The result was: (a) the Gospel of John emphasizes the innocence of Pilate more than any of the other New Testament Gospels; (b) hand in hand with this it incriminates the Jews most over their responsibility for the death of Jesus.

Anti-Judaism as an element in a historical description of the activity of Jesus

No wonder, then, that Jesus' controversy with the Jews runs like a scarlet thread through the Gospel of John. This controversy comes to a head where Jesus describes the Jews as sons of the devil (John 8.44). From the beginning, the author of the Gospel of John emphasizes the Jews' intention to kill Jesus: 5.16, 18; 7.1; 8.19; 8.22–24, 37–59. It is continued in 10.31–39; 11.45–53; 19.7. The embittered dispute reaches a provisional climax in 8.37–45. It had begun in 2.14, and extends over many disputations up to 8.59.

The anti-Judaism of the Gospel of John is thus an ingredient of a historical description of the activity of Jesus. Here is the most important extract from it.

John 8.37–45:

'37 I know that you are sons of Abraham; yet you seek to kill me, because my word finds no place in you. 38 I speak of what I have seen with my Father, and you do what you have heard from your father.' 39 They answered him, 'Abraham is our father.' Jesus said to them, 'If you were Abraham's children, you would do what Abraham did, 40 but now you seek to kill me, a man who has told you the truth which I heard from God; this is not what Abraham did. 41 You do what your father did.' They said to him, 'We were not born of fornication; we have one Father, even God.' 42 Jesus said to them, 'If God were your Father, you would love me, for I proceeded and came forth from God; I came not of my own accord, but he sent me. 43 Why do you not understand what I say? It is because you cannot bear to hear my word.

44 You are of your father the devil, and your will is to do your father's desires. He was a murderer from the beginning, and has nothing to do with the truth, because there is no truth

in him. When he lies, he speaks according to his own nature, for he is a liar and the father of lies.

45 But, because I tell the truth, you do not believe me.'

In this text the unbelieving Jews are explicitly termed children of the devil or sons of the devil. The controversy between the Christians behind the Gospel of John and the unbelieving Jews comes to a climax which can hardly be surpassed. Without doubt the sharpness of the polemic can be explained from the fact that Christians from the association of Johannine communities and unbelieving Jews have clashed. To this degree the statements here are conditioned by their time. However, they are hardly rhetorical, nor are they even a play on words. The author doubtless means what he writes and writes what he means. And that means that the unbelieving Jews are demonized in the text. This demonizing does not necessarily presuppose a great historical distance between them and the Johannine community. Indeed this may be a dispute within Judaism, which only later led to a final separation. Controversies between groups which are internally close are always sharper than those between parties which are not interested in each other. But this does not in any way alter the finality of the condemnations uttered (*pace* Thyen 1980).

Anti-Judaism in the framework of Johannine theology

If a sharp anti-Judaism was already developing in the historical account of Jesus' activity, it is expressed more intensely in Johannine theology. The Jews have a significant place in the framework of Johannine dualism. Here we have the contrast between God and world, light and darkness, truth and lie, in which as representatives of the world Jews stand for those who do not believe. They belong to darkness (8.12), the lie (8.44) and death (8.51): they are 'of this world' and come 'from below' (8.23). They have not recognized the one who who is 'from above' and 'not from this world', and so they must die in their sins (8.24). 'In taking offence at the fact that he calls God his Father and makes himself equal with God (5.18), that he claims to be before Abraham (8.58; cf. 8.53), they indicate that they do not know where the Revealer comes from or where he is going (7.33f.; 8.14)' (Strecker 1995: 520). They do not know God (5.19–47; 7.28; 15.21; 16.3), indeed they cannot know him, since God is known only through the Son (8.14,19,42). Because they 'judge according to the flesh' (8.15), they abide in unfreedom; for only the Son makes people really free (8.33ff.). 'If salvation also comes from the Jews (4.22), this applies only in a provisional sense, related to the historical experience of Jesus; for true worship is offered in the spirit and in truth (4.23)' (Strecker 1995: 520).

The other side of this abrupt anti-Judaism lies in the Gospel's christology, as is shown for example in John 14.6: 'I am the way, the truth and the life; no one comes to the Father but by me.' Now this claim to exclusivity is utterly Jewish. It is rooted both in Jewish exclusivism (see Ch.2) and in the bitterness of intra-Jewish controversy (see 113 above).

The Revelation of John

The Revelation of John presents itself as letters 'to the seven churches in Asia' (1.4), but according to 1.2 can be aptly characterized throughout as the account of a vision. The author calls himself John (1.1, 4, 9; 22.8), and seems to be a highly-respected figure among those whom he addresses. He introduces himself as a prophet (1.9–20; 22.7, 10, 18f.). His writing was probably composed during the persecution under the emperor Domitian (81–96), but perhaps only under the emperor Trajan (98–117).

Revelation 2–3 contains seven letters of the risen Christ to churches in Asia Minor; we must assume that they are authentic despite their uniform structure. 'Authenticity' means that John composed them and attributes their content to the risen Christ (cf. Rev. 1.19). The letters give information about the conditions in the various churches and at two points make negative statements about unbelieving Jews.

Letter to the church of Smyrna (Rev. 2.9)

In the letter to the church of Smyrna, in Rev. 2.9 we read: 'I know your tribulation and your poverty (but you are rich) and the slander of those who say that they are Jews and are not, but are a synagogue of Satan.'

The author disputes that another group should be called Jews and describes their members abruptly as a synagogue of Satan. He claims the name of Jews for himself and his church. The word 'synagogue' suggests that this is a Jewish group. Its members were evidently in dispute with John's church over the question of the Messiah and thus over the christological confession. John regards the denial that Jesus is the Messiah as blasphemy. He adopts the standpoint of the Christian churches from the second generation on, who – whether Gentile or Jewish Christians – denied that any Jews who refused to believe in Christ were members of the people of God. With the expression 'synagogue of Satan' the risen Christ challenges the claim of the Jewish community to be an assembly (= synagogue) of God (cf. Num. 16.3). That happens because 'the Jews have refused to recognize him as ruler of the people of God. And according to the historical view of Revelation, which tends towards dualism, anyone who does not submit to the rule of Jesus Christ, and thus of God, surrenders himself to the rule of God's demonic adversary' (Roloff 1984: 52).

It remains open whether a complete separation between John's church and the local Jewish synagogue has taken place. The Jewish character of Revelation tells against this; the harshness of the polemic suggests it. However, it is clear that whether or not a complete separation has yet taken place, it is imminent.

Letter to the church of Philadelphia (Rev. 3.9)

In the letter to the church of Philadelphia, in Rev. 3.9 we read: 'Behold, I will make those of the synagogue of Satan who say that they are Jews and are not, but lie – behold, I will make them come and bow down before your feet, and learn that I have loved you.'

In this letter the risen Christ speaks through John in the same way as he does in the letter to the church of Smyrna. Here too he denies real Jews the honorific title of Jews. It has often been thought that at this point, as in the letter to the church of Smyrna, the term 'Jew' denotes Jewish-Christian Gnostics who have appeared within the churches. But the praise of the church in Philadelphia in Rev. 2.8b tells against this: 'You have kept my word and have not denied my name' rules out serious disturbances in church life at that time (cf. Lohse 1992: 6). Now if the Gnostic thesis is ruled out for Rev. 3.9, by virtue of the identical expressions the same is true for Rev. 2.9.

We must conclude that in both places the risen Christ alias John denies (unbelieving) Jews the honorific name of Jews because they will not agree with his christology or attack it. The polemic is sharp, but not unusual within Judaism, as the following examples attest:

(a) The Qumran community, which observed the law strictly, condemned all other groups of Judaism who took obedience to the will of God less seriously or followed a different interpretation from theirs: 'They are a congregation of wickedness, and all their works are in darkness' (1QM XV,9); the sons of darkness 'do wickedness against the covenant' (1QM I,2), they are 'an assembly of deceit and a congregation of Belial (= Satan)' 1QH II,22). The 'congregation of God' (1 QM IV,9) must resist them in steadfast loyalty and must be ready to fight against them (cf. Lohse 1992:21).

(b) According to Jubilees 15.33, all Jews who do not have their children circumcised are 'sons of Beliar (= Satan)'.

(c) However, the polemical statement about being a synagogue of Satan is not as unusual as appears at first sight. For the Christian communities, too, continue to be endangered by Satan (cf. Rev. 2.13, 24).

But reflections on the possible historical proximity of the Christian church to the Jewish synagogue cannot alter the rigorous language in any way. Here too anti-Judaism is grounded in christology, as it is in the Gospel of John.

Interim reflection

It is now time to ask whether the content of the text from Eusebius's *Church History* quoted at the beginning of this chapter corresponds to what the New Testament authors have said about the Jews. Is the religiously motivated repudiation of the Jews in Eusebius to be identified with that of the New Testament authors?

This question calls for a positive answer. First, both Eusebius and the synoptic Gospels present the destruction of Jerusalem as God's punishment for the murder of Jesus. Secondly, on each occasion the repudiation of the Jews is grounded in christology. Thirdly, despite their deep roots in Jewish traditions, like Eusebius the New Testament authors cited leave no doubt that their Christian confession is complete and does not need to be supplemented. They represent a closed system which does not allow openness to those who believe otherwise, however closely related these may be. Indeed, it almost seems as if precisely because of their tragic (!) proximity to Jews who do not believe in Christ, the New Testament writers make even more radical condemnations of their Jewish contemporaries than Eusebius. In addition we should note that these partly devastating statements are attributed to Jesus himself and thus are given an unassailable authority.

The origin of anti-Judaism in the New Testament

It is possible to make well-founded statements about the origin of anti-Judaism. It is directly bound up with the claim of the Christian communities that salvation is only in Christ and in no one else. Cf. Acts 4.12 (Peter's sermon): 'And there is salvation in no one else, for there is no other name under heaven given among men by which we must be saved.' In other words, christology leads to a claim which excludes all other ways of believing, and if it is not acknowledged, it immediately vilifies this way. Cf. further John 14.6: 'I am the way, the truth and the life, no one comes to the Father but through me.' In addition it should be noted that anti-Judaism arose only when the church was predominantly Gentile Christian. For example christology presented within Judaism, as for example in the case of Bar Kochba, who at the beginning of the second century was declared to be Messiah by Rabbi Akiba (cf. Karrer 1991: 316–19; Schäfer 1981: 55–67), knew no anti-Judaism.

Now the two texts mentioned (and others which are not cited here) are rooted in a particular situation and are not meant to be judgments which apply in all situations and at all times, nor were they meant to be accepted into a canon of sacred writings. Rather, they can be explained historically. Given their content, the only possibility is to understand them in the light of the claim to exclusiveness made by the groups concerned or by the Christianity which handed down these judgments. Any other understanding would go against their literal content. In other words, in their view there is no getting round an acknowledgment of Jesus Christ as the salvation of the world – either for the Jews or for the Gentiles, regardless of whether their author was still a member of a Jewish community or already outside it. And if – as often happened – Jews and/or Gentiles did not assent to this judgment about Jesus as salvation of the world, they *had to* be assigned to the realm of darkness. So anti-Judaism is the other side of 'Christ alone'; in Rosemary Ruether's term, anti-Judaism is the left hand of christology (Ruether 1976; for the discussion of her important book in North America cf. the contributions in Davies 1979 and the elucidations in Gager 1983: 13–34 and Klassen 1986: 16–18).

It has been said of this thesis that 'in a way it fixes the New Testament to its later history of anti-Jewish exegesis ... without taking seriously the distinctions and especially the qualitative change in the relationship between Christians and Jews which is beyond question there, the development which took place as a result of the parting of the ways at the end of the first centuries and above all in the centuries which followed' (Stegemann 1980: 120). This objection needs only to be set against the substance of the New Testament evidence for us to see that it is inadequate, though it must immediately be acknowledged that at various times anti-Judaism had more than one cause. One need think only of a possible influence of pagan antisemitism on the early Christians or of their persecution by Jewish authorities. Here more reflection is needed, taking special geographical peculiarities into account. But none of this alters the general correctness of the judgment that the Jews were lambasted by the New Testament authors with anti-Jewish language because they did not accept the confession of Christ.

So Ulrich Wilckens is right in judging: 'We cannot get avoid recognizing that all the early Christian writings are steeped in a more or less sharp opposition to surrounding Judaism' (1974: 604). This verdict can be extended further to the opposition also to paganism, from which the early church strictly marked itself off, simply because of the monotheism it had taken over from Israel.

Possibilities of correcting anti-Judaism?

It is all too understandable that, given this evidence which is so comfortless for present-day Jewish-Christian dialogue, the view has been expressed that anti-Judaism must not be the left hand of christology (cf. Marquardt 1983: 9). Rather, the task consists in finding a christology which affirms Israel (ibid).

However, in view of the New Testament texts which have been analysed above, this call must be termed illusory. At the same time it should be emphasized that this christology affirming Israel existed only in that Jewish Christianity outside the New Testament which was vilified by the mainstream church (cf. Lüdemann 1996: 52–60). The earliest Christian romance, the Pseudo-Clementine *Homilies*, a romance about recognition and reunion, which in its final form comes from the fourth century but which contains traditions from the early Christian period, includes the requirement that the Hebrews (= Jews) must obey the teaching of Moses, and Christians the preaching of the true prophet Jesus, if they want to be blessed (*Hom.* VIII 5–7). The teaching of Moses is said to be identical with that of Jesus; Jesus is said to be veiled from the Hebrews, whereas Moses is hidden from those who believe in Jesus *(Hom. VIII 6, 1–2)*.

However, in antiquity this Jewish Christianity could not achieve a majority or make itself plausible; it was wrongly vilified, and exercised no further influence on the historical development. Rather, the Gentile Christianity of the second century, taking New Testament statements further, referred the election of Israel to itself and in connection with this, again as a result of christology, formally tore the Old Testament out of the hands of the unbelieving Jews.

Is the kind of approach represented in vilified Jewish Christianity possible today? Thus we can repeatedly read: 'Jews and Christians walk in the name of God, the former listening to the word of the Torah, the latter bound to Jesus Christ' (von der Osten-Sacken 1982: 186). However, that would mean breaking away from almost all the New Testament tradition, for 'there is no way of liberating Christianity from its anti-Judaism without finally struggling with its christological hermeneutic' (Ruether 1978: 112). Since von der Osten-Sacken arrives at his solution by means of dogmatics, i.e. on the basis of the existing New Testament material, and with no reference to heretical Jewish Christianity, exegetically this solution does not have a chance, however much the wish for a reconciliation between Jews and Christians which underlies it is to be affirmed. The same applies to the latest 'christology', which has the same concern. Here it is abruptly decreed: 'Jesus of Nazareth is none other than the risen Jesus Christ' (Marquardt 1990: 132), and the resurrection is again regarded as a historical event (Marquardt 1991: 284). Given the state of the sources, this makes a dialogue almost impossible. Thus no true understanding between Jews and Christians can be arrived at through dogmatics. Once the advocates of a lasting closer relationship between Israel and the church referred to the vilified Jewish Christians, it would immediately be necessary to offer a critique of the New Testament canon, and at present I can see no signs of this in the circles around von der Osten-Sacken and Marquardt.

But the reference to the *one* God as the strongest bond

between Israel and the church is hardly a solution of the problem addressed either. For the confession of the one God, which would also have to include Islam, is empty until the content of this confession becomes clear and understandable. 'The Jewish confession of the one God cannot be detached from its awareness of being the one chosen people. The Christian confession of the one God cannot be detached from the one Son in whom God has reconciled the world to himself' (Grässer 1985: 314). This verdict is certainly true on the basis of the final form of the New Testament texts.

A solution to the problem by means of a reconstruction of Christian origins?

Now beyond doubt the two key texts which have been quoted, Acts 4.12 and John 14.6, come only from the time after the destruction of the Jerusalem temple in 70 CE. Is it not possible that only then did christology lead to anti-Judaism, whereas the first Christians and their view of Christ was free of this? The answer to this must be negative. (a) Already in the earliest extant letter of Paul, I Thessalonians, from either 41 or 50, Paul launches sharp attacks on the Jews who killed the Lord Jesus (I Thess. 2.15). (b) Furthermore, reference must be made to serious controversies between Jews and Jewish Christians in the first years of the existence of the Jerusalem community, as a result of which the Hellenistic Jewish Christians of Jerusalem around Stephen had to leave the city (Acts 6–7; on the historical questions behind Acts 6–7 see Lüdemann 1989: 73–93). The Hellenists were quite sure that they were the new people of God, in which only the Christians (Jews and Gentiles) had a place. Cf. the baptismal formula which Paul probably received from these circles, Gal. 3.28: 'There is neither Jew nor Greek ... all are one in Christ.' This understanding of the church, which as in Paul (see above, 84f.) might originally have come close to a restoration of the original spiritual Judaism, very soon, partly due to the dynamic of Gentile Christian self-assertion, led to a substitution theory. The church has succeeded to Israel.

A participation model or a substitution theory in the understanding of the church?

In the early period of Christianity, only the Jerusalem community may have thought differently about the relationship between the church and Israel and have advocated a participation model (instead of a substitution theory). According to this view, the Christians have a share in the privileges of Israel (cf. Luz 1981: 202). This is indicated first by the evidence that the Gentile mission was accepted only grudgingly by the Jerusalem community and immediately had obligations imposed upon it (cf. Lüdemann 1996: 44–49). Secondly, through the collection for the Jerusalem community the Gentile Christians received a share in its status – at any rate, this is the standard interpretation of the collection by the Jerusalem community (cf. Lüdemann 1996: 47f.). This would then have put a brake on anti-Judaism, as one would also infer from the christology of the vilified Jewish Christians who were the descendants of the Jerusalem community. In neither case would there be any threat to Israel, as the Gentiles would have no status independent of it.

In general Paul himself advocates a substitution model, but later adds to this the mystery of the hope for the redemption of the whole of Israel (cf. Rom. 11.26). Thus if we take note of the historical context of this statement, he prevented *ad hoc* any anti-Judaism on the part of the Gentile Christians of Rome. But this solution is in tension with other statements in his letters, with which a balance cannot immediately be achieved. Thus Paul understands the church as the Israel of God (Gal. 6.16) and thinks that the wrath of God has already come upon the Jews who are a hindrance to his Gentile mission (I Thess. 2.16). Moreover, his practice in fact destroys the Jewish identity, as his Jewish Christian opponents rightly observed. One of his principles, which goes back to the traditions that he received from the Hellenists, was: 'For neither circumcision counts for anything nor uncircumcision, but keeping the commandments of God' (I Cor. 7.19); and another: 'For neither circumcision counts for anything, nor uncircumcision, but a new creation'

(Gal. 6.15). Sooner or later these polemical formulae necessarily caused the Jewish Christians living in Paul's communities as a minority to depart from the Torah and cease to have their children circumcised – the very charge that his Jewish Christian opponents had made against the apostle; cf. Acts 21.21: Paul teaches 'all the Jews who are among the Gentiles to forsake Moses, telling them not to circumcise their children ...' So the evidence in Paul is ambiguous: on the one hand the apostle leaves as a legacy an abiding pointer to the roots of the church in Israel. On the other, Paul's work sets off an avalanche in the direction of a purely Gentile Christian church.

But if all the New Testament evidence, with the differentiation that needs to be made in the case of Paul, is clear, at the same time it must be added that the christological and ecclesiological claim was made only after the resurrection of Jesus. Since in terms of content it represents an interpretation of the life and work of Jesus of Nazareth, I would suggest that this insight should be utilized for a new way of dealing with anti-Judaism.

A new way of dealing with anti-Judaism

If anti-Judaism is necessarily the other side of christology, this is a problem which needs to be identified. Here historical criticsm provides invaluable help. It is certain that christology is ultimately rooted in the resurrection of Jesus. But this resurrection never took place; only the visions of disciples can be said to be facts (cf. Lüdemann 1994). If you like to put it that way, the Jews mentioned by Matthew had a more appropriate assessment of the 'resurrection' of Jesus than the early Christians. They gave voice to the nagging suspicion that the disciples had stolen the corpse of Christ (Matt. 28.13–15), whereas the Christians stubbornly claimed that Jesus' body had disappeared from the tomb in Jerusalem. If the Christians did not remove the corpse, it must necessarily have decayed. On this presupposition, but also on others, like a contesting of the virgin birth and the doctrine of the divinity of Christ and his pre-existence, the

Jews were right. So in general it is important to take Jesus himself as the starting point for future theology, however much that may rock the boat of the church. In the case of Jesus of Nazareth, anti-Judaism is *a priori* doomed to failure, since he knew that he had been sent exclusively to his Jewish contemporaries and understood himself to be a reformer of the religion of Israel. In addition, the questions about the Old Testament as the Word of God and as a part of the Bible, which so far have remained open, have to be resolved by his person and preaching.

The tragic side of anti-Judaism

I would like to add two points: (a) anti-Judaism was and is the creeping poison in the history of Christianity. Whether it has already passed its climax in the history of the Christian churches and theology remains to be seen. (b) At the same time anti-Judaism has tragic features, since much in it has in fact been taken over from Israel and later was even turned against the Jews. Part of the real problem seems to be how a people can suddenly claim that it has been chosen and *vice versa*. For election often provokes hostility to the others who have not been chosen. It may also intensify opposition to members of one's own group who seem to be disloyal to its central conviction (cf. Pagels 1995: 15 and the important review article by TeSelle 1996). A number of controversies between Jewish groups can be traced, but the Christians made a permanent division between themselves and other Jews and linked them with Satan and the forces of evil. With the adoption from Judaism of the disastrous legacy of this aspect of religion, along with its concept of God, the *de facto* use of force was programmed into the Christian church, and the war theology of the Old Testament served as a model. To the present day, the image of God in the Christian churches still seems to be heavily stamped by the God of the Old Testament, who makes use of force, and who is to be obeyed without protest. But how can such a God find a home in our democratic traditions and the concept of tolerance which is rooted in them (cf. Mensching 1966; T.Rendtorff 1982)? The question is still unresolved, since neither (a) the Reformation nor (b) more recent mainstream dogmatics in Germany contribute anything to this question.

(a) Martin Luther's intolerance to heretics is expressed crudely, but not inappropriately, in his *Table Talk*: 'One need not waste much time on heretics; one can condemn them unheard. And whereas they perish at the stake, the believer should tear up the evil at the roots, and bathe his hands in the blood of the bishops and the pope, who is the devil in disguise' (III, 175).

Luther's remarks in his *Table Talk* may be coarse and 'easily excusable', but they are an expression of his attitude to those who believe otherwise (for what follows cf. Völker 1912). This can be demonstrated, for example, from Luther's *Greater Catechism*:

> Hence these articles of the Creed divide and separate us Christians from all other people on earth. For those who are outside Christianity, be they heathens, Turks, Jews or false Christians and hypocrites, and although they may believe in only one true God and worship Him, yet they do not know how He feels towards them, and cannot expected either love or any blessing from Him, and accordingly remain in eternal wrath and perdition; for they have not the Lord Christ, and are likewise not enlightened and blessed by any gifts from the Holy Spirit (The Creed, Third Article).

Luther's polemic, which results from his intolerance towards those of other views and convictions, is directed against the Catholic Church (e.g. 'Against Hans Worst', 1541), as against the Turks (e.g. 'On the War against the Turks', 1529), against Reformation heresies, like the Anabaptists and enthusiasts, and also especially against the Jews. For example, in his 1543 work *On the Jews and their Lies*, we can read:

> Such a desperate, thoroughly evil, poisonous, and devil's lot are these Jews, who for these fourteen hundred years have

been and still are our plague, our pestilence, and our mis-
fortune (*Luther's Works* 47, 275).

First, to set fire to their synagogues or schools and to bury or
cover with dirt whatever will not burn, so that no man will
ever again see a stone or cinder of them. This is to be done in
honour of our Lord and of Christendom, so that God might
see that we are Christians, and do not condone or knowingly
tolerate such public lying, cursing, and blaspheming of his
Son and of his Christians...
   Secondly, I advise that their houses also be razed and
destroyed. For they pursue in them the same aims as in their
synagogues. Instead they might be lodged under a roof or in
a barn, like the gypsies. This will bring home to them the fact
that they are not master in our country ...
   Third, I advise that all their prayer books and Talmudic
writings, in which such idolatry, lies, cursing, and blasphemy
are taught, be taken from them.
   Fourth, I advise that their rabbis be forbidden to teach
henceforth on pain of loss of life and limb ... (*Luther's Works*
47, 268f.; cf. 285f.)

For Luther, other views are not only deviations from true
doctrine but are excesses of the devil himself (cf. e.g. the preface
to the Schmalkald Articles, 1537/38): 'How can I alone stop all
the mouths of the devil?', who if need be is even to be fought
with violence (cf. e.g. WA 15, 774).
   The same is true of Philipp Melanchthon. He called the
execution of Michael Servetus in 1553 in Geneva, urged by Jean
Calvin because of Servetus' criticism of the doctrine of the
Trinity, 'a pious example worth remembering by all posterity'
(CR IX, 133). The helpless protest written by the humanist
Sebastian Castellio (1515–1563), which was only published
in 1612 (cf. Bainton 1965), could do nothing against this
intolerance grounded in the idea of God, but at least it should
find a hearing today.
   (b) No less a figure than Karl Barth, who has shaped the

dogmatic theology of this century more than anyone else and continues to affect it, writes: 'No sentence is more dangerous or revolutionary than that God is One and there is no other like Him... Let this sentence be uttered in such a way that it is heard and grasped, and at once 450 prophets of Baal are always in fear of their lives. There is no more room now for what the recent past called toleration. Beside God there are only his creatures or false gods, and beside faith in him there are religions only as religions of superstition, error, and finally irreligion' (Barth 1957: 444). This statement, which was also written against National Socialism, certainly had an important function then; but in a democratic and pluralistic age it is poison for efforts towards an understanding between the different religions, and moreover fails to do justice to the historical conditioning of any human statements, including those about God.

4

Jesus and the Mercy of God

Reflection on Jesus for the purpose of preserving the biblical heritage

If we still want to link up with the biblical heritage and the tradition of its interpretation by the church, it is important resolutely to refer back resolutely to Jesus. This needs to be done for both historical and theological reasons – for historical reasons, because Jesus was *the* catalyst for the Christian movement, and for theological reasons because the significance of his message and his conduct extends to the present day and moreover contains a potential for liberation which can still apply to all men and women. But this claim must first be tested by what Jesus really proclaimed in word and deed and what he did not. We must grapple with the question whether one can understand the person of Jesus without doing him an injustice by our present-day interpretations and the past interpretations coming from primitive Christianity. Theology must allow itself to be measured by the historical Jesus or should immediately become philosophy or a sophisticated doctrinal catechism on an academic basis: confirmation instruction for scholars.

Theses on the words and behaviour of Jesus

I shall sum up my picture of Jesus here in the form of theses. This is how it appears to me from a study of all the Jesus traditions, and it will soon appear in an independent monograph.

At the heart of Jesus' *picture of God* is not the figure of a vengeful, zealous God but one of a God who turns to men and women in mercy, a God who had become unknown to many of Jesus' contemporaries. Jesus' God seeks the lost. These do not first have to decide to repent. Jesus speaks to God as to a dear Father, and his talk of faith, which presupposes the Old Testament concept of the faithfulness of God, includes the unconditional certainty that faith is no longer an errant longing but rests on God. If in the Old Testament faith was also orientated on a picture of God as a successful warrior for Israel (cf. Isa. 7.9 [in the Syro-Ephraimite war], 'If you do not believe you will not be established'), for Jesus it is orientated on individuals and the unconditional promise of salvation to them, and on the experience of healing of body and soul.

Jesus' *preaching* is orientated on non-violence and on love of enemy, which mixes up the existing order and breaches the principle of retribution regardless of its effect. Jesus understands, measures and lives out the tradition of love that first allows us to live in a human way, open to the world and indeed reasonably, in the freedom of the children of God, and to remain true to his creation. His teaching is focussed on the belief that the traditional norms are there for human beings and not vice versa. Therefore Jesus often deliberately became a lawbreaker and had the courage to criticize openly.

In his *behaviour* Jesus distances himself from the ruling classes and turns towards those who have no religious status: toll collectors, prostitutes, the people of the land who are ignorant of the law. In so doing he demonstrates clearly that grace falls upon men and women – without any kind of claim.

Jesus' *fate* was to die a death on the cross because he had made himself unpopular; here he paid the price for the way in which he stood unshakeably by his convictions and for his unconventional behaviour.

Jesus' *expectation* that God's kingdom would arrive in the foreseeable future came to grief. To this degree he failed. When church circles preached the bodily resurrection of Jesus from the dead his message was falsified. He lives on in the sense that his friends handed down his message. Essential parts of his preaching remain valid, even if its eschatological orientation has sunk without trace. Elements of his expectation which have been lost once for all also include that of the new temple, if he really hoped for one, and the restoration of the twelve tribes of Israel, of which he saw the Twelve as representatives.

Jesus did not claim any christological titles for himself. If we are not afraid of modern terms, the designation 'Reform Jew' may be an appropriate one for him. Nevertheless an 'I' shines out which claims an unconditional authority, is bound up with the deity as he understands it in the most intimate way, and appears in the name of that deity. As such a figure, the Jesus who can be reconstructed with historical criticism is a challenge to all men and women. But he is also the criterion for any idea of God and allows, for example, even atheists to identify with him.

The internal context and the starting point of his activity emerge from his relationship with John the Baptist, his teacher. Jesus allows himself to be baptized by John for the forgiveness of sins; here he took the side of sinful humanity and thus *a priori* gave the lie to later christological reflections and statements about his sinlessness. Through being baptized by John he also wanted to avoid the terrible final judgment which the ascetic John threatened on all those who were not ready to repent. Then he parted company with his teacher, ceased to fast, and experienced the rule of God in the present, as it announced itself in exorcisms and other miracles. Jesus used the term 'kingdom of God', which is alien to the preaching of John the Baptist, to denote the time of salvation in which the deity acts in an abundance of grace. Malicious tongues said that Jesus was a glutton and winebibber, a friend of tax collectors and sinners (cf. Matt. 11.19). The grain of truth here is that he also celebrated the dawning kingdom of God in meals with a great host of followers.

The human Jesus – unsuitable for church preaching?

Is not a Jesus understood in this way purely a human being and therefore completely unsuitable to be the Christ of the churches? Anyone who asks this question evidently knows in advance what Christ is suitable for the churches. But that is where the problem lies.

(a) If the Christian churches claim Jesus for themselves, then they must respect Jesus as he really was and recognize the later over-paintings of his preaching and person as later additions; these include (in addition to all the christology) around 85% of all the sayings of Jesus which have been handed down.

(b) Nor should one be deceived about the internal state of the Christian churches today. Many have internally been evacuated of all substance and externally have no credibility.

(c) Even church functionaries no longer believe what is written in the creeds. Thus the President of the Synod of the Evangelical Church in Germany, Jürgen Schmude, recently said in an interview with the journal FOCUS that he believed in the resurrection of Jesus, but immediately added that he had to interpret what that meant (FOCUS 17/1996: 70). What does he really believe? Can I believe in things which I have to interpret afterwards? Either I believe or I don't believe, and we should give an account of this belief to ourselves and others. I conjecture that most church functionaries also want to believe, but confuse this desire with true faith. It is simply absurd to believe in things which have to be interpreted afterwards. The same is also true when giving other, secular, definitions. Thus I cannot say 'I believe in freedom' and only then go on to interpret what is to be understood by that. Freedom is realized in history, and so it is always concrete. It is also there when it exists only as a possibility, in the form of alternative actions. Whereas concrete freedom is clear, interpretations always have an ambiguity about them. It follows from this that I must say what I really believe.

So the fact remains that there are thousands of Christs, i.e. human pictures of a super-earthly Son of God, but only one Jesus. What has largely governed the preaching of the church in the last two thousand years has not been what this Jesus thought, wanted and did, but what was thought about him after his death and done in his name. But the divinized Christ has little to do with Jesus. Many Christians increasingly suspect that today, and many church functionaries have meanwhile become aware of it again. Therefore the statement that 'the skeleton in the closet of the church is the risen Jesus' (Türcke 1996: 144) holds without qualification. We must turn away from this illusion in order to encounter Jesus in honest historical reconstruction and thus be given an opportunity for meaningful life in the third millennium as well.

5

A Criticism of my Church

This chapter is above all a critical contribution to the discussion which has begun in Germany about the legitimacy of radical historical criticism in the framework of academic theology and the church. But it may also be of interest to English readers, since in the Anglo-Saxon world, too, the question of the relationship between history, faith, church and theology has still not been clarified.

1. Never has so much importance been attached to theological education – and never has the Word of God been so lacking in savour, power and fruit as now. The reason for this does not lie with the preachers, who are in the service of the church and are dependent on their employers; for the most part they are men and women of good will. The real reason is the untenability of the supposition that the 'Word of God' is preached from the pulpit at all.

2. The church which bases itself on the Word of God has built on sand. This follows, first, from the history of the canon, i.e. from the human way in which the collection that makes up the Bible, consisting of Old and New Testaments, came into being. Secondly, talk of the Bible as Word of God has become obsolete as a result of the way in which the dogma of inspiration has been taken off its hinges by historical criticism. Thirdly, the unity of the earthly and risen Jesus, which represents an important basis for the notion of the Bible as Word of God, is outdated because the resurrection appearances to his disciples are to be derived from visions which can be explained in purely psychological terms and which can be understood as interpretations of the life of Jesus.

3. The churches should take a creative break, and dispense with preaching the 'Word of God' for at least ten years. Think of all the things that are preached about! If everything preached up and down the country is God's Word, then how are we to explain its almost complete lack of effectiveness?

4. As in all spheres of life, so too in religion, the consequences of this knowledge must be drawn, and if necessary that must lead to its complete transformation. That applies above all to the historical evidence that Jesus decayed and did not rise bodily. For the church, the physical resurrection is nevertheless still an indispensable requisite, so that we can say with Christoph Türcke that the skeleton in the closet of the church is the risen Son of God.

5. Theology and church must be liberated from their entanglements with each other – for the good of theology and for the good of the church. Theology cannot be done as church theology, but only as free, scholarly theology. Only then is it in a position to make its contribution to the demystification of the world. The church is not just based on rationality, but primarily on a religious community experience which takes place at the grass roots. Singing and celebrating has priority there. Only this makes possible the necessary communication with other churches of the ecumene. The church must become more aware of itself; it can make decisions on the basis of its practice and need not artificially resort to theological formulae to demonstrate its orthodoxy.

6. The claim to privileged knowledge is the besetting evil of the theology of both confessions and both churches. This has contributed to their lack of credibility and their speechlessness in dealing with outsiders – who are in the majority. Anyone who refers here to revelation is simply doing what the present-day sects also practise.

7. Protestant theology owes its reputation and its right to

exist within German universities to the ruthless application of historical criticism. Along with many other contemporaries who engaged in historical criticism, a scholar like Adolf von Harnack, who as a culture Protestant and a liberal theologian is no longer taken seriously, did more for the ongoing existence of theological faculties in a secular state (cf. von Harnack 1923) than those in today's church who despise him and his like suspect.

8. Theology and the church will have a right to exist in the future only if they offer the public what is required of them in modern society. Within the framework of a demonstration of the need for them, the historical truth of the statements that they confess in the creed must be tested, and if the result is negative these statements must be firmly dropped. There is no necessity for theology and the church to exist. Theology must again link up with the great historical, philological and philosophical achievements of liberal theology.

9. If theology is to be recognized as an academic discipline there must be an end to its confessionalizing. That should be easier to achieve in Protestantism than in Roman Catholicism. Furthermore this demand needs to be made not only for organizational and economic reasons, but also for political reasons, since our state is confessionally neutral. In the new theological faculty there should be research into all religions including the Christian religion. Though theology and the church actually exist, they do not necessarily have to. All of them should be put to the critical test. Practical training of clergy is a matter for the Christian churches and the other religious communities, and not for the universities.

10. Theology and the church often live on the fact that no one takes them seriously any more. This alone ensures their survival in times which are politically relatively stable, and this survival is secured in law by partisan agreements between state and church. But we should not fool ourselves: for many thinking

people and today's culture, the church and theology are no longer a challenge. They lead a life of their own, often dig themselves in against unpleasant criticism, and thus stiffen into death in apparent splendour.

11. The church is called on to hear Jesus' voice for better or worse in his authentic words. This includes a readiness to distinguish ruthlessly what Jesus really said from what he did not say, and to question one's own tradition in the light of the authentic sayings of Jesus. Here a living memory is more than mere repetition of the words of Jesus.

12. If I am not repudiated by historical evidence or a clear reason, I am compelled by the historical facts that I have cited to maintain my protest against the hypocrisy of the Protestant Church, its confessions which are still pronounced today, and the actions of its officers which are grounded on the 'Word of God'.

Bibliography

To save space, the works cited are quoted in abbreviated form from the start, by the name of the author and the date of the edition used (in the case of translations, dates in brackets refer to the date of the original)

Albert, Hans, *Traktat über kritische Vernunft*, 1968; ²1969
—, *Plädoyer für kritischen Rationalismus*, 1971; ³1973
Albertz, Rainer, *A History of Israelite Religion in the Old Testament Period* (1992), 1994
Alt, Albrecht, 'Die Heimat des Deuteronomiums' (1953), in id., *Kleine Schriften zur Geschichte des Volkes Israel* II, 1953, 250–75
Anders, Günther, *Endzeit und Zeitenende. Gedanken über die atomare Situation*, 1972
Bainton, Roland H., *Concerning Heretics. Whether they are to be persecuted and how they are to be treated. A collection of the opinions of learned men both ancient and modern. An anonymous work attributed to Sebastian Castellio*, 1965
Barr, James, 'The Old Testament and the New Crisis of Biblical Authority', *Interpretation* 25, 1971, 24–40
—, *Biblical Faith and Natural Theology*, 1993
Barth, Karl, *Church Dogmatics* II/1 (1940), 1957
Bauer, Walter, *Orthodoxy and Heresy in Earliest Christianity*, edited and enlarged by Georg Strecker (²1964), 1972
—, *Das Leben Jesu im Zeitalter der neutestamentlichen Apokryphen*, 1909 (= 1967)
Becker, Hans-Jürgen, *Auf der Kathedra des Mose. Rabbinisch-theologisches Denken und antirabbinische Polemik in Matthäus 23, 1–12*, ANTZ 4, 1990
Ben-Chorin, Schalom, 'Antijüdische Elemente im Neuen Testament', *EvTh* 40, 1980, 203–14
Birkner, Hans-Joachim, 'Natürliche Theologie und Offenbarungs-theologie. Ein theologiegeschichtlicher Überblick', *NZSTh* 3, 1961,

279–95

Blenkinsopp, Joseph, *Ezra-Nehemiah. A Commentary*, 1988

Broer, Ingo, '"Antisemitismus" und Judenpolemik im Neuen Testament. – Ein Beitrag zum besseren Verständnis von I Thess 2, 14–16', *BN* 20, 1983, 59–91

—, 'Der Prozess gegen Jesus nach Matthäus', in Karl Kertelge (ed.), *Der Prozess gegen Jesus. Historische Rückfrage und theologische Deutung*, QD 112, ²1989, 84–110

—, 'Antijudaismus im Neuen Testament? Versuch einer Annäherung anhand von zwei Texten (1 Thess 2, 14–16 und Mt 27, 24f)', in Oberlinner, Lorenz and Fiedler, Peter (eds.), *Salz der Erde – Licht der Welt. Exegetische Studien zum Matthäusevangelium (FS Anton Vögtle)*, 1991, 321–55

Brown, Raymond F, *From Gethsemane to the Grave. A Commentary on the Passion Narratives in the Four Gospels* (2 vols), 1994

Buggle, Franz, *Denn sie wissen nicht, was sie glauben. Oder warum man redlicherweise nicht mehr Christ sein kann*, 1992

Bultmann, Rudolf, *The History of the Synoptic Tradition* (1931), ²1968

Conzelmann, Hans, *The Theology of St Luke* (1953), 1960

Crossan, John Dominic, *Who Killed Jesus?*, 1996

Davies, Alan (ed.), *Antisemitism and the Foundation of Christianity*, 1979

Davies, Philip R., 'A Neo-Albrightean School in History and Biblical Scholarship?', *JBL* 114, 1995, 683–705

Dibelius, Martin, *From Tradition to Gospel*, 1934

Dietrich, Walter and Link, Christian, *Die dunklen Seiten Gottes. Willkür und Gewalt*, 1995

Donner, Herbert, and Röllig, Wolfgang, *Kanaanäische und aramäische Inschriften* II, Kommentar, 1964

Ebach, Jürgen, *Das Erbe der Gewalt. Eine biblische Realität und ihre Wirkungsgeschichte*, 1980

Ebeling, Gerhard, *Kritischer Rationalismus. Zu Hans Alberts* Traktat über kritische Vernunft, 1973

Erwachsenenkatechismus, Evangelischer, Kursbuch des Glaubens, produced by the Catechism Commission of the United Evangelical Lutheran Church of Germany and edited by Werner Jentsch, Hartmut Jetter, Manfred Kiessig and Horst Reller, ²1975

Flusser, David, 'Ulrich Wilckens und die Juden', *EvTh* 34, 1974, 236–43

—, 'Das Schisma zwischen Judentum und Christentum', *EvTh* 40, 1980, 214–39

Friedrich, Gerhard, *Die Verkündigung des Todes Jesu im Neuen Testament*, BThSt 6, 1982

Fritz, Volkmar, *Das Buch Josua*, HAT 1/7, 1994

Gager, John C., *The Origins of Anti-Semitism. Attitudes Toward Judaism in Pagan and Christian Antiquity*, 1983

Gevirtz, Stanley, 'Jericho and Shechem: A Religio-Literary Aspect of City Destruction', *VT* 13, 1963, 52–62

Grässer, Erich, *Der Alte Bund im Neuen. Exegetische Studien zur Israelfrage im Neuen Testament*, WUNT 35, 1985

Gunneweg, A. H. J, *Understanding the Old Testament* (1977), 1978

Haacker, Klaus, 'Elemente des heidnischen Antijudaismus im Neuen Testament', *EvTh* 48, 1988, 404–18

Haenchen, Ernst, *Gott und Mensch. Gesammelte Aufsätze*, 1965

—, 'Historie und Geschichte in den johanneischen Passionsberichten', in *Zur Bedeutung des Todes Jesu. Exegetische Beiträge*, Schriftenreihe des Theologischen Ausschusses der Evangelischen Kirche der Union, ed. Fritz Viering, ²1967, 55–78

Harenberg, Werner, 'Detektive in Höhle 7', *Der Spiegel* 22/1996, 64–87

Harnack, Adolf von, 'Die Bedeutung der theologischen Fakultäten', in id., *Erforschtes und Erlebtes*, 1923, 199–217

Harnisch, Wolfgang, '"Toleranz" im Denken des Paulus? Eine exegetischhermeneutische Vergewisserung', *EvTh* 56, 1996, 64–82

Heckel, Martin, *Die theologischen Fakultäten im weltlichen Verfassungsstaat*, 1986

Herrmann, Siegfried, 'Die Abwertung des Alten Testaments als Geschichtsquelle. Bemerkungen zu einem geistesgeschichtlichen Problem', in Hans Heinrich Schmid and Joachim Mehlhausen (eds.), *Sola Scriptura. Das reformatorische Schriftprinzip in der säkularen Welt*, 1991, 156–65

Hirsch, Emanuel, *Geschichte der neueren protestantischen Theologie im Zusammenhang mit den allgemeinen Bewegungen des europäischen Denkens*, I, ³1964

Hirschler, Horst, *Luther ist uns weit voraus*, 1996

Janowski, Bernd and Welker, Michael, 'Vorwort', in *Jahrbuch für Biblische Theologie* 1,1986, 5–8

Jeremias, Joachim, *The Parables of Jesus*, 1972

Julicher, Adolf, *Die Gleichnisreden Jesu*, ²1910 (=1963)

Kaiser, Otto, *Isaiah 1–12*, OTL (1960), 1973

—, *Einleitung in das Alte Testament. Einführung in ihre Ergebnisse und Probleme*, [4]1978

—, *Isaiah 1–12* (new edition), OTL (1981), 1983

—, *Grundriss der Einleitung in die kanonischen und deuterokanonischen Schriften des Alten Testaments. Band 1: Die erzählenden Werke*, 1992

Kampling, Rainer, *Das Blut Christi und die Juden. Mt 27,25 bei den lateinischsprachigen christlichen Autoren bis zu Leo dem Grossen*, NTA 16, 1984

Kampling, Rainer, 'Eine auslegungsgeschichtliche Skizze zu 1 Thess 2,14–16', in Dietrich-Alex Koch and Hermann Lichtenberger (eds.), *Begegnungen zwischen Christentum und Judentum in Antike und Mittelalter (FS Heinz Schreckenberg)*, 1993, 184–213

Kang, Sa Moon, *Divine War in the Old Testament and in the Ancient Near East*, BZAW 177, 1989

Kant, Immanuel, *Schriften zur Anthropologie, Geschichtsphilosophie, Politik und Pädagogik. Erster Teil*, Werke in sechs Bänden, 6, 1966

Karrer, Martin, *Der Gesalbte. Die Grundlagen des Christustitels*, FRLANT 151, 1991

Kilian, Rudolf, *Jesaja 1–39*, EdF 200, 1983

Kittel, Gerhard, 'Das Konnubium mit Nicht-Juden im antiken Judentum', *FJF* 2, [2]1943, 28–59

Klappert, Berthold, 'Zur Erneuerung des Verhältnisses von Juden und Christen, I. Einführung, II. Synodalbeschluss zur Erneuerung des Verhältnisses von Christen und Juden', *EvTh* 40, 1980, 257–76

Klassen, William, 'Anti-Judaism in Early Christianity: The State of the Question', in Richardson and Granskou 1986,1–19

Klein, Charlotte, *Theologie und Anti-Judaismus. Eine Studie zur deutschen theologischen Literatur der Gegenwart*, ACJD 6, 1975

Klein, Günter, 'Christlicher Antijudaismus. Bemerkungen zu einem semantischen Einschüchterungsversuch', *ZThK* 79, 1982, 411–50

Koch, Klaus, *The Prophets, Vol.2, The Babylonian and Persian Period* (1980) 1983

Koester, Helmut, *Ancient Christian Gospels. Their History and Development*, 1990

Kraus, Hans-Joachim, *Psalmen. 2. Teilband*, BK XV/2, 1966

Kraus, Hans-Joachim, *Die biblische Theologie. Ihre Geschichte und Problematik*, 1970

Kümmel, Werner Georg, *The New Testament. A History of the*

Investigation of its Problems (1970), 1973

—, *Das Neue Testament im 20.Jahrhundert. Ein Forschungsbericht,* SBS 50, 1970

Kuhn, Karl Georg, 'Theos, C. The Early Christian Fact of God and Its Conflict with the Concept of God in Judaism. 2. The rabbinic terms for God', *TDNT* 3, 1965, 92–4

Lagarde, Paul de, 'Ueber das Verhältnis des deutschen Staates zu Theologie, Kirche und Religion. Ein Versuch Nicht-Theologen zu orientieren', in id., *Deutsche Schriften. Gesamtausgabe letzter Hand,* ⁵1920, 40–83

Leipoldt, Johannes, and Morenz, Siegfried, *Heilige Schriften. Betrachtungen zur Religionsgeschichte der antiken Mittelmeerwelt,* 1953

Lemche, Niels Peter, *Early Israel. Anthropological and Historical Studies on the Israelite Society Before the Monarchy,* SVT XXXVII, 1985

Lémonon, Jean-Pierre, *Pilate et le gouvernement de la Judée. Textes et monuments,* FtB, 1981

Lescow, Theodor, 'Das Geburtsmotiv in den messianischen Weissagungen bei Jesaja und Micha', *ZAW* 79, 1967, 172–207

Levine, Amy-Jill, *The Social and Ethnic Dimensions of Matthean Social History. 'Go nowhere among the Gentiles' (Matt. 10:5b),* SBFC 14, 1988

Ley, Michael, *Genozid und Heilserwartung. Zum national-sozialistischen Mord am europäischen Judentum. Mit einem Vorwort von Leon Poliakov,* ²1995

Lindemann, Andreas, 'Jesus blieb im Grab', *Deutsches Allgemeines Sonntagsblatt* 7/1994, 17

Lohfink, Norbert, 'Das heutige Verständnis der Schriftinspiration in der katholischen Kirche', in Eckert, Willehad P., Levinson, Nathan P., and Stöhr, Martin (eds.), *Antijudaismus im Neuen Testament?,* ACJD 2, 1967, 15–26

Lohse, Eduard, *Synagoge des Satans und Gemeinde Gottes. Zum Verhältnis von Juden und Christen nach der Offenbarung des Johannes. Franz-Delitzsch-Vorlesung* 1989, 1992

Lüdemann, Gerd, *Paulus und das Judentum,* TEH 212, 1983

—, *Early Christianity according to the Traditions in the Acts of the Apostles. A Commentary* (1987), 1989

—, *The Resurrection of Jesus. History, Experience. Theology,* 1994

—, *Heretics. The Other Side of Early Christianity* (1995), 1996

Luz, Ulrich, 'Zur Erneuerung des Verhältnisses von Christen und Juden. Bemerkungen zur Diskussion über die Rheinländer Synodalbeschlüsse', *Jud.* 37, 1981, 195–211

—, 'Der Antijudaismus im Matthäusevangelium als historisches und theologisches Problem. Eine Skizze', *EvTh* 53, 1993, 310–27

Marguerat, Daniel, 'Juden und Christen im lukanischen Doppelwerk', *EvTh* 54, 1994, 241–64

Marquardt, Friedrich-Wilhelm, *Die Gegenwart des Auferstandenen bei seinem Volk Israel. Ein dogmatisches Experiment*, ACJD 15, 1983

—, *Das christliche Bekenntnis zu Jesus, dem Juden. Eine Christologie*, 1, 1990; 2, 1991

Meinhold, Peter, *Ökumenische Kirchenkunde. Lebensformen der Christenheit heute*, 1962

Mensching, Gustav, *Toleranz und Wahrheit in der Religion*, 1966

Meyer, Eduard, *Ursprung und Geschichte der Mormonen*, 1912

Mormon, The Book of, translated into English by Joseph Smith Jr (1830), 1948

Mussner, Franz, *Tractate on the Jews* (1979), 1983

Newport, Kenneth G. C., *The Sources and Sitz im Leben of Matthew 23*, JSNT.S 117, 1995

Nietzsche, Friedrich, *Works*, Complete Translation, 1911

Noth, Martin, *Überlieferungsgeschichtliche Studien*, 1943 (=1963)

Origen, *Der Kommentar zum Evangelium nach Matthäus III*, eingeleitet, übersetzt und mit Anmerkungen versehen von Hermann J. Vogt, BCrL 38, 1993

Osten-Sacken, Peter von der, *Grundzüge einer Theologie im christlich-jüdischen Gespräch*, ACJI 12, 1982

Overbeck, Franz, *Zur Geschichte des Kanons*, 1880 (= 1968)

Pagels, Elaine, *The Origin of Satan*, 1995

Pannenberg, Wolfhart, 'The Crisis of the Scripture Principle' (1962), in id., *Basic Questions of Theology*, 1970, 1–14

Pannenberg, Wolfhart, *Theology and the Philosophy of Science* (1973), 1976

Perlitt, Lothar, 'Israel und die Völker', in Liedke, Gerhard (ed.), *Frieden–Bibel–Kirche*, 1972, 17–64

—, *Deuteronomium-Studien*, FAT 8, 1994

Preuss, Horst Dietrich, *Theologie des Alten Testaments, 1, JHWHs erwählendes und verpflichtendes Handeln*, 1991

Provan, Iain W, 'Ideologies, Literary and Critical: Reflections on

Recent Writing on the History of Israel', *JBL* 114, 1995, 585–606

Rad, Gerhard von, *Studies in Deuteronomy* (1948), 1953

—, *Holy War in Ancient Israel* (1958), 1991

Reimarus, Hermann Samuel, *Apologie oder Schutzschrift für die vernünftigen Verehrer Gottes,* edited on behalf of the Joachim-Jungius-Gesellschaft der Wissenschaften Hamburg by Gerhard Alexander, I, 1972a; II, 1972b

Reinhold, Wolfgang, *Der älteste Bericht über den Tod Jesu. Literarische Analyse und historische Kritik der Passionsdarstellungen der Evangelien,* BZNW 69, 1994

Renan, Ernest, *Histoire du peuple d'Israel,* 1, 1887

Rendtorff, Rolf, 'Die jüdische Bibel und ihre antijüdische Auslegung', in id. and Stegemann, 1980, 99–116

—, *The Old Testament. An Introduction* (1983), 1985

—, and Stegemann, Ekkehard (ed.), *Auschwitz – Krise der christlichen Theologie. Eine Vortragsreihe,* ACJD 10, 1980

Rendtorff, Trutz (ed.), *Glaube und Toleranz. Das theologische Erbe der Aufklärung,* 1982

Reventlow, Henning Graf, *The Authority of the Bible and the Rise of the Modern World,* (1984), 1985

Richardson, Peter and Granskou, David (eds,), *Anti-Judaism in Early Christianity. Volume I: Paul and the Gospels,* SCJud 2, 1986

Römer, Thomas, *Dieu obscur. Le sexe, la cruauté et la violence dans l'Ancien Testament,* 1996

Roloff, Jürgen, *Die Offenbarung des Johannes,* ZBK. NT 18, 1984

Ruether, Rosemary, *Faith and Fratricide. The Theological Roots of Antisemitism,* 1974

Sanders, Jack T., *The Jews in Luke-Acts,* 1987

Schäfer, Peter, *Der Bar Kokhba-Aufstand,* TSAJ 1, 1981

Schürer, Emil, *History of the Jewish People in the Age of Jesus Christ,* ed. G.Vermes and F.Millar, Vol.1, Edinburgh 1973

Slenczka, Reinhard, *Kirchliche Entscheidungen in theologischer Verantwortung. Grundlagen – Kriterien – Grenzen,* 1991

Smend, Rudolf, *Zur ältesten Geschichte Israels,* Gesammelte Studien 2, BEvTh 100, 1987

—, *Die Entstehung des Alten Testaments,* ⁴1989

—, *Epochen der Bibelkritik,* Gesammelte Studien 3, BEvTh 109, 1991

Speyer, Wolfgang, *Bücherfunde in der Antike. Mit einem Ausblick auf Mittelalter und Neuzeit,* Hyp. 24, 1970

—, *Die literarische Fälschung im heidnischen und christlichen Alter-*

tum. Ein Versuch ihrer Deutung, HKAW 1, 2, 1971
—, 'Religiöse Pseudepigraphie und literarische Fälschung im Altertum'
(1965/66), in Brox, Norbert (ed.), *Pseudepigraphie in der heidnischen und jüdisch-christlichen Antike*, WdF CDLXXXIV, 1977,
195–263
Spieckermann, Hermann, *Juda unter Assur in der Sargonidenzeit*,
FRLANT 129, 1982
Stegemann, Ekkehard, 'Der Jude Paulus und seine antijüdische
Auslegung', in Rendtorff and id., 1980, 117–39
—, ' Zur antijüdischen Polemik in I Thess 2,14–16', *Kirche und Israel*
5,1990, 54–64
Stiegler, Stefan, *Die nachexilische JHWH-Gemeinde in Jerusalem*,
1994
Stöhr, Martin, 'Einführung', in W. P. Eckert, N. P. Levinson and id.
(eds.), *Antijudaismus im Neuen Testament?*, ACJD 2, 1967, 7–14
Strecker, Georg, 'Die Leidens- und Auferstehungsvoraussagen im
Markusevangelium (Mk 8,31; 9,31; 10,32–34)', in id., *Eschaton
und Historie. Aufsätze*, 1979, 52–75
—, *Theologie des Neuen Testaments*, revised, enlarged and edited by
Friedrich Wilhelm Horn, 1995
Synode der Evangelischen Kirche in Deutschland, *Glauben heute.
Christ werden – Christ bleiben. Mit einem Brief an alle, denen der
Glaube und die Kirche am Herzen liegen und dem Vortrag Die
Entdeckung des Glaubens im Neuen Testament von Professor Dr.
Hans Weder*, 1988
Te Selle, Eugene, 'Demonizing the Powers: Pagels' *Origin of Satan* in
Context', *RSR* 22, 1996, 2–9
Theissen, Gerd, 'Aporien im Umgang mit den Antijudaismen des
Neuen Testaments', in *Die hebräische Bibel und ihre zweifache
Nachgeschichte (FS Rolf Rendtorff)*, ed. Blum, Erhard, Macholz,
Christian, and Stegemann, Ekkehard W., 1990, 535–53
Thiede, Carsten Peter, *The Earliest Gospel Manuscript: Qumran
Fragment 7QS and its Significance for New Testament Studies*,
Carlisle 1995
Thyen, Hartwig, 'Exegese des Neuen Testaments nach dem Holocaust', in Rendtorff and Stegemann 1980, 140–58
Türcke, Christoph, *Kassensturz. Zur Lage der Theologie*, 1992
—, 'Die Leiche im Keller. Christentum und ethischer Minimalkonsens
heute', in *Das Christentum am Ende der Moderne*, 1996
Völker, Karl, *Toleranz und Intoleranz im Zeitalter der Reformation*,

1912

Wagner, Falk, *Zur gegenwärtigen Lage des Protestantismus*, 1995
Weatherly, Jon A., *Jewish Responsibility for the Death of Jesus in Luke-Acts*, JSNT.S 106, 1994
Wegner, Reinhard (ed.), *Die Datierung der Evangelien*, ²1983
Weippert, Manfred, '"Heiliger Krieg" in Israel und Assyrien. Kritische Anmerkungen zu Gerhard von Rads Konzept des "Heiligen Krieges im Alten Israel"', *ZAW* 84, 1972, 460–93
Wellhausen, Julius, *Skizzen und Vorarbeiten* I, 1884
—, *Das Evangelium Johannis*, 1908
—, *Das Evangelium Matthaei*, ²1914
—, *Israelitische und jüdische Geschichte*, 1958
Wilckens, Ulrich, 'Das Neue Testament und die Juden', *EvTh* 34, 1974, 602–11
Windisch, Hans, *Johannes und die Synoptiker. Wollte der vierte Evangelist die älteren Evangelien ergänzen oder ersetzen?*, UNT 12, 1926
Winter, Paul, 'Markus 14,3b.55–64. Ein Gebilde des Evangelisten', *ZNW* 53, 1962, 260–3
—, 'Zum Prozess Jesu', in Eckert, Willehad P, Levinson, Nathan P. and Stöhr, Martin (eds.), *Antijudaismus im Neuen Testament?*, ACJD 2, 1967, 95–104
—, *On the Trial of Jesus*, Second Edition. Revised and edited by T.A. Burkill and Geza Vermes, SJ 1, 1974
Würthwein, Ernst, *Die Bücher der Könige (1. Kön 17–2. Kön. 25)*, ATD 11, 2, 1984
Zager, Werner, 'Jesu Auferstehung – Heilstat Gottes oder Vision? Das Ostergeschehen in historisch-kritischer und psychologischer Perspektive', *Deutsches Pfarrerblatt* 96, 1996, S. 120–3
Zeller, Eduard, *Die Philosophie der Griechen in ihrer geschichtlichen Entwicklung* III.2, ⁶1963
Zimmerli, Walther, *Man and His Hope in the Old Testament* (1968), 1971

Appendix: Ideologies, Text and Tradition[1]

John Bowden

Christians and Jews both have Bibles. Moreover they both have traditions of interpreting their Bibles as texts, in all kinds of ways. However, Jews and Christians also use, or have used their Bibles as history books, and have taken over the histories recounted in their Bibles as part of the histories of their respective faith communities.

Here, though, it is disturbing that these biblical histories of faith communities continue to be used quasi-fundamentalistically after there has been a revolution in the way in which we understand history writing, and we have developed a historical consciousness.

It is generally recognized that we can no longer use the Bible as a scientific textbook, though in Christianity until past the end of the first millennium of the Common Era it was thought to be just that. I would argue that it can no longer be used as a history book either, and that if we are writing the histories of our respective traditions, we need to do so on quite a different basis. However, to accept that revolution would, I suspect, cause such upheavals in our respective communities as to be almost unthinkable. This paper attempts to set out some of the issues.

Most of us probably saw something on television of the student occupation of Tienanmen Square in Peking, and of the brutal way in which that was ended. We saw with our own eyes the hospitals to which the wounded and the dead were taken and the fear stalking the corridors. So when we were told by the Chinese authorities that there had been no massacre, that this was not a legitimate protest, and so on, we were totally disbelieving. We did not accept that the authorities were speaking the truth.

Similarly, all of us are appalled that right-wing neo-Nazi groups in Germany and elsewhere claim that there were no death camps in Hitler's Germany, and that the destruction of six million Jews and others was a figment of the imagination, a myth. Obviously, even the young outsider who reads Martin Gilbert's book on the Holocaust or sees Lanzmann's film *Shoah*, and hears the testimony of survivors, knows that this kind of history is not true.[2] To be told that there were no death camps is to be told lies.

We are aware that the lies which we are told in this way are told for a purpose. They are told to justify and defend a particular ideology, a particular view of society and the world, which needs for its support and continuance to describe reality in a particular way – and if reality does not fit the ideology, so much the worse for reality. In the instances I have taken we have an ideological Chinese Communist view of history and a Fascist view of history, but these views lie outside what would be regarded as true history by the scholarly world.

We do recognize that there is truth and falsehood in history writing, that history can be manipulated, and that it is also possible to know when history is being manipulated. The distinction between truth and falsehood is easiest to see when we are told that we did not see what we did see or experience what we are experiencing. This distinction becomes less easy the further back in time we go, and in events and periods which can be approached from different, yet related perspectives. Sometimes we may be reduced to not knowing precisely what happened. I am not suggesting that anyone can write objective history, but we do know that we need to watch out for ideology, and it can be identified when it plays an excessive role.

History is manipulated now, and we may also legitimately assume *a priori* that, since it is unlikely that ours is the first century in which history-writing has been manipulated, it will have been manipulated in the past.

Now, as I have indicated above, we know that in the way that we look at history we are different from most of those who came before us. Our understanding of history, the way in which we approach the writing of history, what can be called our historical consciousness, is essentially a result of developments in the nineteenth century. Along with the insights symbolized by Marx and Freud, those of nineteenth-century historians, followed by twentieth-century sociologists, have led to a whole paradigm shift in the way in which we look at past and present. We are conditioned by our history and our culture, but we also *know* that we are conditioned by our history and our culture, a situation which can often give us almost split personalities. However, the important thing is that we can recognize that our attitudes are different from those of our predecessors, who were not aware of what we now call historical and cultural relativity. The people of the ancient world, for example, were not just people like us wearing different dress and without the benefits of technology. They *were* different. And our awareness of that is something that makes us what we are.

Secondly, there is a *moral* dimension in our view of what happened in Tienanmen Square and Auschwitz and the way in which it is reported or not reported. We believe that – to put it mildly – the extermination of Jews was wrong; we believe that the massacre of student protesters was wrong. And we believe it is wrong to say that these things did not happen if we know they did. Ask us *why* we know that it is wrong and you hit on one of the great unanswered questions of our age – the nature and basis of moral judgments in a pluralist society – but that is not my particular concern here. We do accept, in our society, that these things are wrong. And here, too, we know that things have not always been this way.

For in times past, massacre, genocide, extermination have, horrifically, been carried out time and again for the sake of some alleged 'higher' end – usually religion, often used as a veneer on economic expansion and imperialism. Think of the peoples of Africa and Latin America who were exterminated – and are still often mercilessly exploited – without a further thought. We have a moral sense, and though the world may not be getting any better, our moral sense is certainly developing, forced by the pressure of events to take in, for example, in an unprecedented way a concern for what most of us now feel to be an immoral treatment of the animal world and the environment.

So, to sum up what I am setting out as a starting point.
1. We can recognize truth and falsehood in history writing.
2. Falsehood, particulalyr as justification for immoral actions, offends our moral sense.
3. We recognize that our attitude differs from that of others in other times.

That is *our* attitude; it is what makes us what we are, and while we can further refine it, correct it or develop it, we can only do so within limits; otherwise we remove ourselves from a whole area of social communication and move into 'a world of our own'. As we might do, for example, if we became fundamentalists.

So what do we do about the so-called conquest of Canaan described in the book of Joshua? We are scandalized at those who, when confronted with genocide or massacre, produce an account which denies that such things happened. But how do we cope with a group which, as a majority of scholars would argue, did not experience or perpetrate any massacre on a large scale or genocide and yet claimed that it *did*?

We shall return to this problem later; for the moment it is a good illustration of my concern. Jews – and Christians to an even greater degree – all too often seem to start from the Bible as it is, basically accepting the story that it tells as a reasonably reliable account of the facts, and go on from there, without realizing the questions they beg, the half-truths they perpetrate, the moral issues which they raise and the flimsiness of the theology which they subsequently construct. Here, since I am a Christian, I shall concentrate on the Christian attitudes.

The reason why Christians treat the Bible *as history* the way they do is because they basically trust it. For the greater part of Christian history there was no reason why Christians should not have trusted the Bible, and indeed it was the foundation of all their knowledge. A great many people who are not aware of the problems involved still trust the Bible in this way, with varying amounts of qualification or reservation. But if we take history seriously, particularly the history of biblical study over the past 350 years, we also have to take into account the rise of a scientific approach based on methodological *mistrust*, and the fact that in too many areas the Bible, like other areas of Christian theology, has actually failed to stand up to the trust that Christians, rightly or wrongly, had put in it.

The story of the impact of geographical and scientific studies on the understanding of the Bible from the seventeenth century on and how it led to a shift in presuppositions by the time of the philosopher Spinoza is a familiar one.[3] Roughly speaking, the development could be described like this: up to Spinoza, an attempt was made to see the Bible as truth, by which all else was judged; from that point on the criteria for determining what was truth lay outside the Bible, and the Bible was judged by what seemed to be the truth on the basis of these criteria from outside it. The criteria kept changing, and the questions put to the Bible became increasingly complex and sophisticated, as did the answers given, but the principle remained the same.

This shift in approach has so far not made the impact on Christian theology that it should have done, largely because of the climate in Christian theology until very recently. Most of the Christian books on the history of Israel and the history of Jesus and the early church, theology and biblical studies which have been written so far have been written as it were from within the church to an audience also presupposed to be within the bounds of the church, often making a series of assumptions as to what the reader will already know and accept. And for a long period that was not an unreasonable assumption to make. There *was* a church audience in the broad sense, and a reasonable part of it was literate. However, changes in society – the great drop in churchgoing, cuts in the church's programme of education by the closure of many of its colleges, and so on – have removed much of that audience. Not all is negative, though; on the other hand a significant number of people who would not claim to be church members *are* interested in making sense of their cultural and religious heritage, and in finding out more about it.

What this means is that the horizons within which the Bible and Christianity (and other religions) are studied are now very much wider. To quote the Finnish New Testament scholar Heikki Räisänen:

> To confine oneself to serving a church is – to exaggerate only slightly – comparable to a social scientist's or a historian's confining himself to serve a certain political party (or a certain nation) with his research. It is hard to see much difference in principle between a historian committed to a party and an exegete committed to a church. In both cases a broader perspective seems desirable, a synthesis directed to the wider society.[4]

Against that background, I shall now go on to substantiate the main point which I made at the beginning, namely that it is time to start abandoning, as a basic framework for our understanding of Christianity, the 'history' which Christians have used almost from the start: the Old Testament narrative, the Gospel narrative, Acts and the *Church History* of Eusebius of Caesarea. That is so because it is now possible to see that this is an ideology, party history which does not fall within the canons of what is acceptable history for us.

Here are the problems which arise for me: I shall take them in chronological order, beginning with the Hebrew Bible, the Old Testament.

In describing the history of the people of Israel which provides the background to the birth of Jesus of Nazareth, it is still customary for Christians to use the outline of the Old Testament. Of course some parts of it – for example the creation narratives – are understood with a degree of modern sophistication, and there will be a recognition that the historical value of the accounts up to, say, the time of King David is not as good as that of later accounts. But pick up any history of Israel, even the more 'radical' ones, and you will still see the sequence: patriarchs, exodus, settlement and judges, David and Solomon, divided monarchy, exile and so on. After a rather dark tunnel period there is then a period up to the first century of our era where all accounts are, methodologically speaking, much better, because there is no strait-jacket of a biblical narrative but a variety of sources, and biblical history overlaps with classical history. But then, with Jesus and the early church, we are again focussed upon the biblical framework. Despite all the scepticism over the possibility of writing a life of Jesus, most histories would give the account of that life some shape based on the Gospel record, following it with an account of the spread of Christianity based mainly on Acts, and when Acts gives out there is the *Church History* of Eusebius of Caesarea, who carries the story on to the time of the emperor Constantine. And since these sources – Old Testament, Gospels and Acts, Eusebius – are used so widely, it is difficult to avoid taking over at least some of their value judgments too.

It is natural to use these sources – after all, in most instances they are all we have – but they *are* confessedly partisan writing, and the motives which led to their composition also led to their selection of some material and omission of others, perhaps even to the creation of events which never happened and developments which never took place.

Now my question is – to repeat it once again: can we take over these histories (even in what on the surface looks quite a modern, scholarly way) and use them as *our* history of the periods concerned, claiming that as *our* history, what we take over does not fall victim to the claim, which I began by discussing, that this is not 'true' history? May it not be that in future what we have to do is to look at these histories as the way in which other people ('they') once interpreted their religious beliefs, ask what it might have been like to have been people with views like that, and then work out on quite a different basis how we ourselves carry on the tradition and use the material that has been handed down to us?

If Christians are trying to construct the process by which there arose within Judaism a movement sparked off by Jesus of Nazareth which in due course gave rise to a new religion called Christianity, which by the time of Constantine had gained the endorsement of the Roman emperor, do they not distort that process if they basically go by what the sequence of Old Testament, Gospels and Acts, Eusebius tells them? Are they not trapped into a supposed series of events and interpretations of those events which give us a blinkered view?

As we saw, in the past Christians were forced to learn that their view of the origins of the world, the nature of the universe, the history of the human race and the interrelationship of its peoples, even details of the history of Israel, the life of Jesus and the early church was biassed and in some cases downright wrong. Can we be sure that our process of discovery has gone far enough? May not the time now have come for Christians to stop pretending that the frameworks I have mentioned, within which they customarily work, are ideologies and cannot serve *for us* as histories of our traditions?

The German philosopher Ernst Troeltsch, still a much-underestimated figure, once said of the nature of modern historical criticism: 'The historical method, once it is applied to biblical scholarship and church history, is a leaven which transforms everything and which finally causes the form of all previous theological methods to disintegrate.'[5] He also remarked: 'Give historical method your little finger and it will require your whole hand',[6] adding wryly that in that respect it resembled the devil. Perhaps those sayings are now, belatedly, coming into their own.

One of the most important books to have been written on the Hebrew Bible recently is Giovanni Garbini's *History and*

Ideology in Ancient Israel.[7] Garbini is Professor of Semitic
Philology in the University of Rome, essentially a philologist
and archaeologist with a specific interest in the history of Israel,
and is neither Jew nor Christian, but part of the wider circle of
ancient historians. Though the views which he expresses may
seem to be extreme, they are by no means idiosyncratic or
unfounded. I have talked about his book with several of my
friends who teach Hebrew Bible or Semitics in English universities, and they tell me that they would go along with most of his
decidedly anti-establishment views.

Garbini argues in his first chapter that it is impossible to write
a history of Israel. His main reason is that we can no longer
trust the outline of that history offered to us by the Old
Testament/Hebrew Bible, and since that outline is all we have,
and evidence apart from it is sparse, a history is impossible. 'An
inadequate history is better than no history at all' often seems
to be the reaction of biblical scholars and their readers, but
Garbini points out that *for us* to accept the Old Testament
history is to accept being manipulated – the point I brought out
right at the beginning. There is nothing new, he argues, about
asserting that the Old Testament offers a series of reflections by
Israel on its history rather than the history of Israel; however, it
must be stressed that these are not so much historical reflections
(though sometimes they are that too) as theological reflections.
That means, he argues, that *for us* the value of the Old
Testament as a historical source is very relative, and that a
particular piece of information cannot be considered reliable
until it has been confirmed from elsewhere.

The Old Testament puts forward distinctive theological
points of view, not least in its history writing. And, Garbini
adds,

> The authors of the biblical text knew very well what they
> were doing. When the 'Deuteronomistic historian' (or who-
> ever) treats the Hebrew monarchy in the way with which we
> are familiar we can affirm that he is choosing and co-
> ordinating certain objective data with a view to a certain

thesis. The kings were substantially the same, but chronology, undertakings, affinity and dynasty could be manipulated at will; if a ruler was forgotten it was possible to invent another one.[8]

What makes his detailed study of parts of the Old Testament so damning is the way in which time and again he points out that either:

1. We have no evidence for what the Old Testament says;
2. There are indications that what the Old Testament says has been fabricated in one way or another.
3. New archaeological evidence is accumulating to suggest that what is said in the Old Testament and what is accepted by scholars may be quite untrue.

For example: the glorious empire of David and Solomon may well be largely fiction. In a whole chapter discussing specific evidence Garbini points out that not only does the general picture that we can create from archaeology indicate that it is highly improbable that an empire as great as that depicted in the Old Testament could have existed at that period; the internal evidence of the Bible also puts many question marks about it; David's kingdom is likely to have been much more limited.[9] In other words, a similar view to what is now quite widely accepted about the 'conquest' of Palestine, that it was a minor process of local settlement, needs also to be adopted over David's empire. Moreover, Solomon's glory may well have been projected on to him, for ideological reasons, by attributing to him activities which archaeology suggests were carried on much later, in the time of king Uzziah/Azariah, 'the leper king', the near contemporary of Isaiah.

Garbini concludes:

A critical examination of the biblical text and the use of external data radically modify the picture that the Old Testament presents of the tenth century BC. David never killed Goliath, never knew Hiram of Tyre, never fought against the Idumaeans, Ammonites, Amalekites and

Aramaeans and did not create an empire. If we are to believe
the biblical text he fought only the Philistines and the
Moabites and managed to establish himself as a ruler in
Jerusalem after fighting against Saul, a king in whose service
he previously was. His son Solomon, who succeeded in pre-
serving his father's small state, built a palace for himself with
a small temple for the dynastic god as an annex, but he did
not marry any daughter of Pharaoh, did not enrich himself
with international trade, and was also in all probability forced
to suffer the military expedition of Pharaoh Sheshonk.[10]

More disturbingly for theologians, Garbini has serious
questions about the Old Testament account of the origins of
belief in YHWH, that of an alien body (Yahwistic monotheism)
penetrating and for a long time living alongside an alien culture
(that of Canaan) before finally conquering it (after the exile).

This would be a quite unique development, since in all other
parallel instances of invasions the invaders quite quickly either
impose their religion on the invaded or adopt the invaded's
religion. But – it might be argued – Israelite belief in YHWH
was something quite unique, and therefore might lead to a
unique development. However, it is emerging that belief in
YHWH was not unique. Names in the Old Testament itself
indicate that YHWH was worshipped outside the Israelite
sphere (just one instance is Joram son of the king of Hamath in
II Sam. 8.10); the name occurs at Ras Shamra, Ebla and elsewhere, and an inscription at Khirbet Beit Lei may indicate that
the name *yah* is as generic a term for God as the familiar generic
term *'el*. And what are we to make of the discoveries at Kuntillet
'Ajrud, between the Negeb and Sinai, a ninth/eighth century
prophetic sanctuary with Yahweh being invoked with the god
Bes and a female consort Asherah?[11]

Thus on the evidence, the probability is that the origin of
what we call distinctively Israelite religion is to be dated very
much later than has been supposed, with a prophetic group
much closer to the exile. This could well be confirmed by the
Decalogue, which though allegedly given to Moses and wander-

ing nomads in the wilderness, throughout presupposes life in a settled agricultural society. Indeed in critical scholarship the growing tendency is to put most of the composition of the Old Testament far later than has been previously assumed; more and more of it, from the stories of Joseph and Abraham, to the Deuteronomic literature and the book of Joshua, are being brought past the exile into the post-exilic period. The later the period, the higher the probability of (in our terms) the reading back of ideology into history with the view that this or that *must* have happened.

And now we move on. My further evidence will be presented much more briefly.

On what we know about Jesus I propose to say virtually nothing, because I have written a book on this subject.[12] I am pessimistic about the amount of real historical evidence we can get out of the Gospel material in relation to his person. What needs to be emphasized, though, is the impact of increasing knowledge of the Judaism of the time of Jesus and the increasing collaboration of Jewish and Christian scholars in working on this period in our view of the Gospels.

Something that has become a burning issue for all of us is the recognition of the considerable element of anti-Judaism in the New Testament which colours all its content. Does that not in itself make New Testament history ideological?

To recapitulate some familiar recognitions briefly: We have learned, particularly over the last decade or so, and New Testament scholars have been made to realize, especially by E. P. Sanders' *Paul and Palestinian Judaism*,[13] the degree to which Christians all too often work with a caricature of Judaism which they take no trouble to check out. We are also learning the degree to which the portrayal of the various Jewish groups which appear in connection with Jesus in the Synoptic Gospels is a reading in from a later time which in all probability completely distorts the historical picture of Jesus and the reasons for the subsequent split between Judaism and Christianity.

I quote just two statements:

> When Christianity began, it must have appeared simply as a group of Jews, otherwise generally conforming to the norms of the Jewish populace of Judaea, who had come to believe that the Messiah had come in the person of Jesus ... The Pharisees presumably regarded Jesus as yet another false messiah of a type which was not so unusual in the last days of the Second Temple. Judaism was in what we might call an experimental stage. For this reason, little opposition to the very concept of sectarian divergence existed.[14]

Thus a Jewish scholar, Lawrence Schiffmann. Alongside that, here is the result of a survey made by E. P. Sanders in a book on the significance of Jesus' alleged breaches of the Jewish law:

> Even if each conflict narrative were literally true, it would be seen that Jesus did not seriously challenge the law as it was practised in his day, not even by the strict rule of observance of pietist groups – except on the issue of food. However, the subsequent debate on that issue in the early church makes this the point which may be denied to the historical Jesus with most confidence. He may have been in minor disagreement with one group or another about some legal observances, but prior to the attack on the Temple, I cannot find a single issue which would have been the occasion of a serious charge.[15]

There is no time here to develop this issue at length, but we can at least pause over three consequences which seem to arise from what has been said above.

1. Most of what most New Testament scholars have written about 'the Jews' in Jesus' time and which others still repeat after them is suspect.
2. We do not really know what events or teachings led to Jesus' death.
3. We do not really know what events and teachings led to the split between Judaism and Christianity.

Much work is, of course, going on in this area, but evidence is not plentiful, and, as in any period of antiquity, there are always going to be arguments. But given this situation, surely much of what is said in Christian theology, specifically christology and soteriology, is shown up to be no more than ideology. And where does that leaves us?

We finally come to the Acts of the Apostles and the *Church History* of Eusebius. Much ink has been spilt over how much of Acts is historical and how far it can be verified. However, the most important issue is again the framework in which the various events are set. The significance of a particular happening, the historicity of which in itself can be authenticated, can be changed completely by putting it in a different context. When, for example, was the so-called 'apostolic council' actually held? Paul seems to suggest a different time from that indicated in Acts 15, which could give the council a different significance.

Now the one thing we know about the framework of Acts is that it is essentially straight-line. It carries us through from beginning to end, but we know that it is an over-simplification and it cannot serve as a basis for what we really need, a history of the rise of earliest Christianity. As we all know, Acts is full of loose ends, the existence of which even its author cannot disguise, and raises questions which he does not seek to answer. There are troublesome figures like Apollos, and the disciples in Ephesus who had never heard of the Holy Spirit; we have no idea how Christianity first came to Rome, and so on.

I have linked Eusebius of Caesarea with Acts because he follows essentially the same kind of method. Just as Luke writes an account of the triumph of the gospel through the figures he selects, so Eusebius writes a history of the divine truth, as it meets resistance, conflict and persecution. There are good guys and bad guys: the good are bishops, Christian teachers and martyrs; the bad are heretics, evil emperors and – of course, sadly and horrifically an inevitable development – the Jews. Again, the ground plan is straight-line and simple.

And of course straight-line and simple ground plans can be

communicated very well. They are easily remembered and are extremely influential. But they have their victims. The first and main victim, of course, is the truth. The simple approach fails to represent the complexity of events as they were. If we begin by gathering the abundant evidence, more readily available than most historical evidence, about the diversity of Christianity in the early period, we then get Acts and Eusebius in perspective and see how much is left out. And we may not be so ready to accept their basic presuppositions – on Jews, and also on other unfortunate groups on the margin of what they consider to be Christianity. The good/bad, orthodox/heretic distinctions are judgments after the event by the winners. We are seeing a major reassessment of Gnosticism; we are also seeing a major reassessment of Arius, at the same time as the doctrinal positions of the so-called church fathers are coming under major criticism as a result of the application of doctrinal criticism.[16] Here too, it is sheer ideology to go on repeating what past figures have said. We need to take a new orientation.

But could our respective faith communities as we know them take such a change? At present that seems highly unlikely, indeed wishful thinking. But if we leave all these questions on one side as though they were not there, what are we doing? Given the kind of world in which we live, if we live within a particular area of social communication which regards the asking of this kind of question as legitimate, perhaps even normative, then on what grounds and at what point do we say 'No, you can't ask that?' Is not the point at which we say that the point at which our beliefs become an ideology and we shut ourselves off in our own particular closed circle?

The Christian tradition to which I belong has, among other things, a long and honourable history of engaging boldly with the current scientific, historical, philosophical, intellectual developments of the day, and once it ceases to do that, surely it becomes something other than it has been. But that may be happening.

Notes

1. This hitherto unpublished paper was originally written for a Jewish-Christian dialogue group which met at the Sternberg Centre, Finchley, London between 1983 and 1991 and delivered in March 1990. The membership, nature and history of the group are chronicled in Tony Bayfield and Marcus Braybooke (eds.), *Dialogue with a Difference. The Manor House Group Experience*, London 1992.

2. See Martin Gilbert, *The Holocaust. The Jewish Tragedy*, London 1986; Claude Lanzmann, *Shoah. The Text of the Film*, New York 1985.

3. See e.g. Klaus Scholder, *The Birth of Modern Critical Theology*, London 1990.

4. Heikki Räisänen, *Beyond New Testament Theology*, SCM Press 1990, 95.

5. Ernst Troeltsch, 'Über historische und dogmatische Methode in der Theologie', *Gesammelte Schriften* 2, Tübingen 1913, 730.

6. Ibid., 734.

7. Giovanni Garbini, *History and Ideology in Ancient Israel*, London and New York 1988.

8. Ibid., 14.

9. Ibid., 21–32.

10. Ibid., 31f.

11. Ibid., 59.

12. John Bowden, *Jesus: The Unanswered Questions*, London 1988.

13. E.P. Sanders, *Paul and Palestinian Judaism*, London and Philadelphia 1977.

14. Lawrence F.Schiffmann, 'At the Crossroads: Tannaitic Perspectives on the Jewish-Christian Schism', in E.P. Sanders (ed. with A.I. Baumgarten and Alan Mendelson), *Jewish and Christian Self-Definition* Vol.2, *Aspects of Judaism in the Graeco-Roman Period*, London 1981, 115–56: 147f.

15. E.P. Sanders, *Jewish Law from Jesus to the Mishnah*, London 1990, 96.

16. See here the now much-neglected writings of Maurice Wiles, *The Making of Christian Doctrine*, Cambridge 1967; *The Remaking of Christian Doctrine*, London 1974; *Working Papers in Doctrine*, London 1976.

Index of Modern Scholars

Select Index of Biblical References

Old Testament